IDEA® Picture Dictionary 2

An IDEA Language Development Resource

Ballard & Tighe

Brea, California

Language Development Consultants

Patrice S. Gotsch, M.A.T., received a bachelor of arts degree in speech communications from The George Washington University and a master of arts in teaching with a concentration in TESOL from The School for International Training. She has taught ESL/EFL to children and adults in the United States and Japan. She currently develops instructional materials for K-12 students.

Laurie Regan, M.A., received her bachelor of arts and master of arts in English from the University of California, Santa Barbara and the University of California, Davis, respectively. She has contributed to the development of a wide range of educational materials, including authoring *Will a Parrot Eat a Carrot?* and co-authoring *Carousel Connections*. She has worked with students of all ages and is currently teaching creative writing at the elementary school level.

Barbara M. Linde, M.A. Ed., received a bachelor of arts in elementary education from Holy Family College, Philadelphia, Pennsylvania, and a master of arts in teaching with a concentration in reading improvement from the California State University, Northridge. As a reading specialist, she has worked closely with ESL and classroom teachers to provide instruction for ELL students. She taught ESL at the adult level and has also been an adjunct instructor at Old Dominion University, Norfolk, Virginia. Barbara currently develops instructional materials for K-adult programs.

Consulting Educational Specialists

The *IDEA Picture Dictionary 2* greatly benefited from the educators who carefully reviewed the dictionary and provided helpful comments and suggestions.

Gilda Bazan-Lopez, Educational Consultant, Houston, Texas
Nicole Woodson Blair, ESL Specialist, Kansas City, Missouri
Joyce Cockson, Reading Specialist, Omaha, Nebraska
Lisa Kelly, National Board Certified Teacher, Elementary, Alexandria, Virginia
Dr. Joyce Lancaster, Educational Consultant, Tampa, Florida
Dr. Christine Meloni, Associate Professor of English as a Foreign Language, Washington, D.C.
Lauren Nguyen, Instructional Coordinator, Houston, Texas
Nikki Stathis, Educational Consultant, Victorville, California
Dr. Constance Williams, Educational Consultant, Menlo Park, California
Dr. Heping Zhao, Associate Professor of English, California State University, Fullerton, California

Acknowledgments

The publisher thanks the following people for their contributions in the development of the *IDEA Picture Dictionary 2*: David Vigilante, Associate Director of the National Center for History in the Schools, University of California, Los Angeles, for his thorough review of the United States Presidents appendix; Elaine Kapusta, Ann Stekelberg, and Edward Swick for their helpful suggestions; and Dr. Norma Inabinette and Bonnie McKenna for their work on the *IDEA Picture Dictionary 1*.

An IDEA® Language Development Resource

Managing Editor: Dr. Roberta Stathis
Project Editor: Allison Mangrum
Editorial Consultant: Jill Kinkade
Editorial Staff: Kristin Belsher, Nina Chun, Heera Kang, Leslie Ley, and Sean O'Brien
Proofreader: Christine Hood
Art Director: Liliana Cartelli
Desktop Publishing Coordinator: Kathleen Styffe
Desktop Publishing Assistant: Ronaldo Benaraw
Printing Coordinator: Cathy Sanchez

Third Printing
ISBN 1-55501-522-0   Catalog #2-062

IDEA® Picture Dictionary 2

Contents

How to Use This

These are **guide words**. Guide words tell you the first and last words defined on the page.

The words are in **ABC order**.

abandon / achieve

abandon: (uh-BAN-dun) *v.* to leave someone or something.

The sailors must **abandon** the ship before it sinks.

abolish: (uh-BAHL-ish) *v.* to do away with; to put an end to.

The 13th Amendment **abolished** slavery in the United States.

abolitionist: (a-boh-LISH-shuhn-ist) *n.* a person who worked to end slavery.

This is a **word**.

Abolitionists such as Frederick Douglass spoke out against slavery.

about: (uh-BOWT) *prep.* relating to.

This book is **about** caring for a new puppy.

above: (uh-BUHV) *prep.* over or higher than.

This is a **picture** that helps explain the word.

The Statue of Liberty holds a torch **above** her head.

8

absorb: (uhb-ZOHRB) *v.* to take in; to soak up.

The sponge will **absorb** all of the water.

accuse: (uh-KYOOZ) *v.* to blame someone for doing something wrong.

John's sister **accused** him of eating the last cookie.

achieve: (uh-CHEEV) *v.* to do something until it is complete.

You must work hard to **achieve** your goals.

Sounds Like Fun!

Which words on the page have five syllables? Three syllables? Two syllables?

This is a **definition**. The definition tells you the meaning of the word.

4

Dictionary

This is the **phonetic spelling** of the word. It shows you how to say the word. (See pages 6 and 7 for the Pronunciation Key.)

acid / adequate

Aa

acid: (A-sid) *n.* a substance that has a sour taste.

Lemons contain a lot of **acid**.

acre: (AY-kur) *n.* a unit of land equal to 43,560 square feet.

The farm is on hundreds of **acres** of land.

across: (uh-KRAHS) *prep.* on the other side.

She sat **across** from him as they talked.

act: (akt) 1. *n.* a law. 2. *v.* to carry out an action; to perform.

1. Great Britain passed the Stamp **Act** to tax paper goods in the American colonies.

2. In the play, they **acted** angry.

activate: (AK-tuh-vayt) *v.* to turn on; to make something work.

The scientist **activated** the robot.

This is the **part of speech** of the word.

addition: (uh-DISH-shun) *n.* adding two or more num... come up with a sum.

Using **addition**, we know th...

Parts of Speech

In language, we put words into categories in order to better understand their purpose. The following categories can be found in this dictionary:

n. **noun**—person, place, or thing (boy)

v. **verb**—an action by the noun (cut)

adj. **adjective**—a description of the noun (huge)

adv. **adverb**—a description of the verb (occasionally)

prep. **preposition**—a word that shows the relation of a noun or pronoun to other words in the sentence (around)

Her height is not **adequate** for this ride.

This is a **sentence** that includes the word.

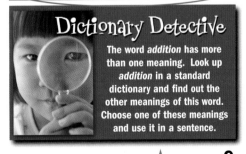

Dictionary Detective

The word *addition* has more than one meaning. Look up *addition* in a standard dictionary and find out the other meanings of this word. Choose one of these meanings and use it in a sentence.

9

This is a **fun activity** for you to try.

Here's the Key!

Each dictionary has a guide or pronunciation key to help readers understand how to say words correctly. The pronunciation key for the *IDEA Picture Dictionary 2* appears below and on page 7. It is a phonetic pronunciation guide. This means that you can learn how to say a word by reading the sounds the letters make. Look at the example to see how this pronunciation key works.

Example:

The letters in parentheses show the phonetic pronunciation for the word *baby*:

baby: (BAY-bee) *n.* an infant or newborn child.

The letter "B" is the first sound in the word *bee*.

The "AY" is the sound you hear in the word *cake*.

The letters "ee" make the sound you hear in the word *key*.

The part of the word—the syllable—written in capital letters tells you to emphasize that syllable. In the word *baby*, you would stress the first syllable ("BAY").

Using this pronunciation key is an easy and fun way to learn how to pronounce words correctly. You can say all the words in this dictionary if you have the key!

VOWEL SOUNDS

A

SYMBOL	KEY WORDS	
a	ant	
ay	cake	
ah	clock	
aw	ball	
ayr	hair	

E

SYMBOL	KEY WORDS	
e	bed	
ee	key	

I

SYMBOL	KEY WORDS	
i	chick	
iy	tiger	

O

SYMBOL	KEY WORDS	
oh	coat	
oo	boot	
oi	boy	
ohr	door	
ow	owl	

U

SYMBOL	KEY WORDS	
u	foot, bird	
u	chicken	
uh	bug	
uh	kangaroo	

International Phonetic Alphabet

ă	ant	ŏ	clock
ā	cake	ō	coat
âr	hair	ô	ball
ĕ	bed	o͝o	foot
ē	key	o͞o	boot
ĭ	chick	ou	owl
ī	tiger	ŭ	bug
oi	boy	ə	chicken; kangaroo

6

CONSONANT SOUNDS

SYMBOL	KEY WORDS		SYMBOL	KEY WORDS	
b	bee		r	roof	
ch	chin		s	saw	
d	doll		sh	sheep	
f	fish		t	toe	
g	goat		th	Thursday	
h	hat		th	mother	
j	juice		v	van	
k	cat		w	water	
l	lip		wh	white	
m	map		y	yellow	
n	nail		z	zebra	
ng	king		zh	television	
p	pail				

NOTE: The pronunciation key is derived from the following three sources: *American Heritage Dictionary of the English Language, 1981; Oxford American Dictionary: Heald Colleges Edition, 1982; Webster's New World College Dictionary, Third Edition, 1990.*

7

abandon: (uh-BAN-dun) *v.* to leave someone or something.

The sailors must **abandon** the ship before it sinks.

abolish: (uh-BAHL-ish) *v.* to do away with; to put an end to.

The 13th Amendment **abolished** slavery in the United States.

abolitionist: (a-boh-LISH-shuhn-ist) *n.* a person who worked to end slavery.

Abolitionists such as Frederick Douglass spoke out against slavery.

about: (uh-BOWT) *prep.* relating to.

This book is **about** caring for a new puppy.

above: (uh-BUHV) *prep.* over or higher than.

The Statue of Liberty holds a torch **above** her head.

absorb: (uhb-ZOHRB) *v.* to take in; to soak up.

The sponge will **absorb** all of the water.

accuse: (uh-KYOOZ) *v.* to blame someone for doing something wrong.

John's sister **accused** him of eating the last cookie.

achieve: (uh-CHEEV) *v.* to do something until it is complete.

You must work hard to **achieve** your goals.

Sounds Like Fun!

Which words on the page have five syllables? Three syllables? Two syllables?

acid: (A-sid) *n.* a substance that has a sour taste.

Lemons contain a lot of **acid**.

acre: (AY-kur) *n.* a unit of land equal to 43,560 square feet.

The farm is on hundreds of **acres** of land.

across: (uh-KRAHS) *prep.* on the other side.

She sat **across** from him as they talked.

act: (akt) 1. *n.* a law. 2. *v.* to carry out an action; to perform.

1. Great Britain passed the Stamp **Act** to tax paper goods in the American colonies.

2. In the play, they **acted** angry.

activate: (AK-tuh-vayt) *v.* to turn on; to make something work.

The scientist **activated** the robot.

addition: (uh-DISH-shun) *n.* the process of adding two or more numbers together to come up with a sum.

Using **addition**, we know that 2+2=4.

adequate: (AD-i-kwit) *adj.* enough to meet a requirement.

Her height is not **adequate** for this ride.

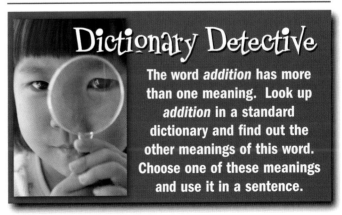

Dictionary Detective

The word *addition* has more than one meaning. Look up *addition* in a standard dictionary and find out the other meanings of this word. Choose one of these meanings and use it in a sentence.

adobe: (uh-DOH-bee) *n.* sun-dried brick made of clay and straw; clay or soil from which such bricks are made.

The Hopi used **adobe** to make their homes.

advantage: (ad-VAN-tij) *n.* something that helps or benefits a person.

Caryn has the **advantage** in this race because she has been training longer than the other swimmers.

advice: (ad-VIYS) *n.* a recommendation about what someone should do.

Greg needed help with his computer, so he called his friend to ask for **advice**.

after: (AF-tur) *prep.* following behind.

Mr. Griffith entered **after** Mrs. Griffith.

against: (UH-genst) *prep.* touching or in contact with something.

He leaned **against** the tree to rest.

agriculture: (AG-ri-kul-chur) *n.* the science of caring for farm land and raising farm animals; farming.

We depend on **agriculture** for our food supply.

airline: (AYR-liyn) *n.* a company that provides travel by air.

The **airline** tries to give great service to its passengers.

airplane: (AYR-playn) *n.* a machine for flying.

Thomas built a toy **airplane**.

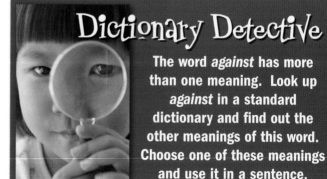

Dictionary Detective

The word *against* has more than one meaning. Look up *against* in a standard dictionary and find out the other meanings of this word. Choose one of these meanings and use it in a sentence.

algae: (AL-jee) *n.* small plants that live in wet areas.

If you do not clean the fish tank often, green **algae** will grow on the sides.

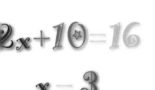

algebra: (AL-juh-bruh) *n.* the part of mathematics that uses letters and other symbols to represent numbers or sets of numbers.

Students use **algebra** to solve mathematical problems.

alike: (UH-liyk) *adj.* similar or the same.

These twins look **alike**.

alligator: (AL-uh-gay-tur) *n.* an animal with a large snout (nose and mouth) and long tail.

Alligators live in swampy places.

almost: (AWL-mohst) *adj.* very nearly.

These animals are **almost** the same height.

along: (UH-lahng) *prep.* over the length of; going in the same direction.

These tall trees are growing **along** the river.

amaze: (UH-mayz) *v.* to impress.

The magician **amazed** the audience with her tricks.

ambulance: (AM-byoo-luns) *n.* a vehicle for carrying sick and injured people to the hospital.

The **ambulance** drove quickly to the hospital.

Aa

amendment: (uh-MEND-munt) *n.* a change to a law or constitution.

The 1st **Amendment** of the U.S. Constitution gives Americans the right to free speech.

amphibian: (am-FI-bee-un) *n.* a type of animal that lives in water when it is young and on land when it is older.

A frog is one type of **amphibian**.

ancestor: (AN-ses-tur) *n.* a person from a family who lived a long time ago.

I researched the lives of my **ancestors** to create our family tree.

ancient: (AYN-shunt) *adj.* very old.

These stones at Stonehenge are **ancient**.

angle: (ANG-gul) *n.* the figure formed by two lines that touch at a point.

We learned to measure **angles** in math class.

angry: (ANG-gree) *adj.* very mad or upset.

This tiger looks very **angry**.

animal: (AN-ni-mul) *n.* a living creature other than a human being.

Many types of **animals** live in the zoo.

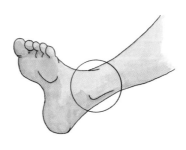

ankle: (ANG-kul) *n.* the joint between the leg and foot.

Your **ankle** helps you move your foot.

announce: (uh-NOWNS) *v.* to say publicly.

Principal Conner **announced** that the football game had been canceled.

ant: (ant) *n.* an insect that lives in an organized group called a colony.

The **ant** is hiding in the grass.

antonym: (AN-ti-nim) *n.* a word opposite in meaning to another word.

"Tall" is an **antonym** for "short."

apartment: (uh-PAHRT-munt) *n.* a set of rooms used as a home.

We live in a two-bedroom **apartment** on the second floor of this building.

apologize: (uh-PAWL-uh-jiyz) *v.* to say one is sorry for something.

He **apologized** to his father for fighting at school.

apple: (AP-ul) *n.* a round fruit.

I ate a bright red **apple** during lunch.

appreciate: (uh-PREE-shee-ayt) *v.* to be thankful or grateful for.

Mr. Franklin **appreciated** Mrs. Miller inviting him on a picnic.

approximately: (uh-PRAHX-i-mit-lee) *adv.* close to; almost.

It is **approximately** 2:30 p.m.

April: (AY-prul) *n.* the fourth month of the year.

Spring flowers grow in **April**.

apron: (AY-prun) *n.* a garment worn to protect clothing.

Wearing an **apron** while you cook will help your clothes stay clean.

aquarium: (uh-KWAYR-ee-um) *n.* a glass tank or bowl in which fish or other water animals are kept.

He keeps his pets in the **aquarium**.

Arabic numeral five

Arabic numeral: (AYR-uh-bik NOO-mur-ul) *n.* the numbers 0, 1, 2, 3, 4, 5, 6, 7, 8, and 9.

The **Arabic numeral** for five is 5.

archaeology: (ahr-kee-AWL-uh-jee) *n.* the scientific study of people and their culture by looking at things they left behind.

In **archaeology**, scientists search for clues to the past by looking at areas where people used to live.

archipelago: (ahr-kuh-PEL-uh-goh) *n.* a group of islands.

The Japanese **archipelago** contains thousands of islands.

architecture: (AHR-kuh-tek-chur) *n.* the style of a building.

You can see several different types of **architecture** in this picture of Florence, Italy.

argue: (AHR-gyoo) *v.* to present reasons for or against something.

Tom **argued** that the school day was too long, but Mara disagreed and said students need to be in school for eight full hours.

aristocracy: (ayr-ris-TAHK-ruh-see) *n.* a government run by the elite or upper class.

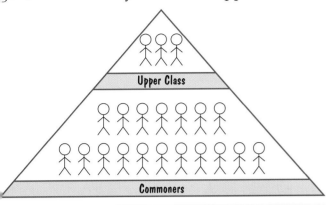

In an **aristocracy**, a small group of people have all the power.

arm: (ahrm) *n.* the upper limb on a person.

His **arm** was tired from cutting the wood.

around: (uh-ROWND) *adj.* in a circle or ring; so as to surround.

The planet Neptune has rings **around** it.

arrange: (uh-RAYNJ) *v.* to place in a desired order.

The florist **arranged** the flowers in a basket.

art: (ahrt) *n.* objects such as paintings, sculpture, and drawings.

"The Mona Lisa" is a famous piece of **art**.

artifact: (AHR-ti-fakt) *n.* an object made by human beings, such as a tool or pottery, that belonged to an earlier time or culture.

The **artifact** we found probably was used for hunting.

artist: (AHR-tist) *n.* a person who practices a fine art such as painting, drawing, or sculpting.

This **artist** likes to paint pictures of the land and sky.

ashamed: (uh-SHAYMD) *adj.* to feel embarrassed and guilty.

Henry was **ashamed** that he broke the planter.

Aa

ask: (ask) *v.* to request information.

Ryan **asked** Nancy to help him with the report.

assassinate: (uh-SAS-uh-nayt) *v.* to murder a political figure.

President Lincoln was **assassinated** in 1865, but his ideas continue to influence people today.

astronaut: (AS-truh-naht) *n.* a person trained for space flight.

The **astronaut** is ready to explore space.

at: (at) *prep.* to be near.

She waited **at** the front door, holding flowers.

atmosphere: (AT-muhs-feer) *n.* the air surrounding the earth.

Pollution in the earth's **atmosphere** is unhealthy.

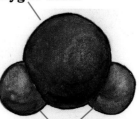

oxygen atom

hydrogen atoms

atom: (AT-um) *n.* the smallest component of an element.

The smallest drop of water is made up of one oxygen **atom** and two hydrogen **atoms**.

audience: (AH-dee-uns) *n.* a group of people watching an event.

The **audience** clapped loudly at the end of the play.

August: (AH-gust) *n.* the eighth month of the year.

August is a summer month.

aunt: (ant) *n.* the sister of one's father or mother.

Baby Sarah loves spending time with her **aunt**.

autobiography: (AH-toh-biy-AH-grah-fee) *n.* a history of a person's life written by that person.

The author wrote about growing up in Africa and moving to the United States in his **autobiography**.

avoid: (uh-VOID) *v.* to prevent from happening.

Some people try to **avoid** getting sick by taking vitamins.

awkward: (AWK-wurd) *adj.* lacking grace; clumsy.

A baby giraffe is **awkward** when it stands and walks for the first time.

axe: (aks) *n.* a tool with a blade for chopping.

You should use a sharp **axe** to chop firewood.

Sounds Like Fun!

There are two "a" words in this dictionary that sound like the same word, but they have different spellings. Can you name them?

Bb

baby: (BAY-bee) *n.* an infant or newborn child.

The **baby** is not old enough to walk and talk.

back: (bak) *n.* the rear part of a person's body.

The man hurt his **back** while lifting the heavy box.

backwards: (BAK-wurdz) *adj.* opposite of the usual or right way.

It was difficult to read the sign because it was **backwards**.

bacon: (BAY-kun) *n.* dried or smoked strips of pork.

Many people cook **bacon** for breakfast.

bacteria: (bak-TEER-ee-uh) *n.* tiny organisms, some of which cause diseases.

You should wash your hands before eating to kill any **bacteria**.

bad: (bad) *adj.* not good.

The newspaper printed a **bad** review of the movie.

badge: (baj) *n.* something worn as a sign of authority or membership.

Officer Martino wears a **badge** to show he is a police officer.

baggage: (BAG-ij) *n.* bags to hold clothes and other personal items while traveling.

Most people bring **baggage** when they travel on an airplane.

baker: (BAY-kur) *n.* a person who makes bread, cakes, and other foods.

The **baker** starts making bread early in the morning.

balance: (BAL-uhns) *n.* the ability to stand up and not fall over.

He needed good **balance** to walk across the wall without falling.

ball: (bawl) *n.* a round object used in games.

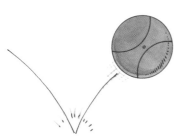

The **ball** bounced on the ground.

ballad: (BAL-ud) *n.* a song, especially one that is romantic or tells a story.

We practiced singing the **ballad** in music class.

balloon: (bu-LOON) *n.* a bag into which air is blown and then used as a toy or decoration.

The child's red **balloon** floated away.

ballplayer: (bawl-PLAY-ur) *n.* a person who plays a sport using a ball.

The **ballplayer** tried to catch the ball.

banana: (bu-NAN-uh) *n.* a long fruit, often with yellow skin.

Tim likes to eat a **banana** for breakfast.

bank teller: (bangk TEL-ur) *n.* a person who works at the counter of a bank.

The **bank teller** gave me money.

Bb

barber: (BAHR-bur) *n.* a person who cuts hair—especially men's hair.

The **barber** cut Miguel's hair.

barn: (bahrn) *n.* a building for storing things such as hay, grain, or livestock.

The farmer put the hay in the **barn**.

bars: (bahrz) *n.* playground equipment for climbing or swinging.

Sam likes to play on the **bars** during recess.

baseball: (BAYS-bawl) *n.* a game played with a bat and a ball.

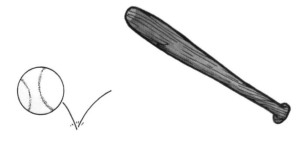

After getting a ball and bat, the children were ready to play **baseball**.

basin: (BAY-sun) *n.* a round container for holding water.

We filled the **basin** with water.

bat: (bat) *n.* 1. a flying mammal with large wings. 2. a long stick used for hitting a ball in the game of baseball.

1. A **bat** can fly in the dark.

2. Heather uses this **bat** when she plays baseball.

bathing suit: (BAY-thing soot) *n.* clothing worn for swimming.

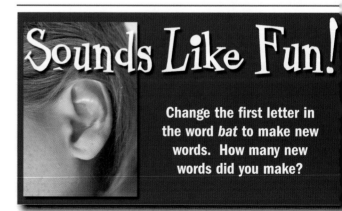

The children brought their **bathing suits** to the beach.

Sounds Like Fun!

Change the first letter in the word *bat* to make new words. How many new words did you make?

20

bathroom: (BATH-room) *n.* a room with a sink and toilet, and sometimes a bathtub or shower.

We brush our teeth in the **bathroom**.

bathtub: (BATH-tuhb) *n.* an area you fill with water and sit in to get clean.

The **bathtub** is filled with water.

bean: (been) *n.* the seed of a plant eaten as a vegetable.

Last night, we ate **beans** and rice for dinner.

bear: (bayr) *n.* a large mammal with thick fur and a very short tail.

On our camping trip, we saw a **bear**.

beautiful: (BYOO-tuh-ful) *adj.* lovely; pretty; nice to look at.

Beautiful flowers bloom in the spring.

beaver: (BEE-vur) *n.* a small mammal with a wide tail and sharp teeth.

The **beaver** picked up a branch by the river.

become: (bee-CUM) *v.* to develop or grow into.

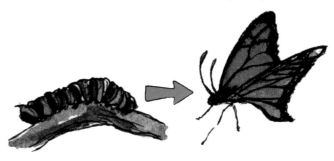

Caterpillars **become** butterflies.

bed: (bed) *n.* a piece of furniture on which people sleep.

I took a nap on the **bed**.

Bb

bedroom: (BED-room) *n.* a room used for sleeping.

The curtains and sheets in my **bedroom** are blue.

bee: (bee) *n.* a yellow and black insect that has wings and makes honey.

The **bee** landed on the flower.

before: (bee-FOHR) *prep.* prior to an event.

She studied **before** the test.

behave: (bee-HAYV) *v.* to act properly.

The man wants his dog to **behave**.

behind: (bee-HIYND) *prep.* on the farther side of; beyond.

He waved from **behind** the tree.

below: (bee-LOH) *prep.* lower than; underneath.

From the sky, the buildings **below** look tiny.

belt: (belt) *n.* a band of leather or material worn around the waist.

You can wear this **belt** with your brown pants.

bench: (bench) *n.* a long, hard seat for several people.

Marco and Heather sat on the **bench** and waited for their turn at bat.

22

Bb

beside: (bee-SIYD) *prep.* next to; near.

She stood **beside** the table.

between: (bee-TWEEN) *prep.* in the space separating two things.

The mother sat **between** her two children.

beyond: (bee-YAWND) *prep.* past; further than.

Our house is **beyond** the white fence.

bicycle: (BIY-sik-ul) *n.* a vehicle with pedals, handlebars, and two wheels; bike.

Courtney rides this **bicycle** to school.

big: (big) *adj.* large.

The man pointed to the bones of the **big** dinosaur.

biography: (biy-AHG-ruh-fee) *n.* the history of another person's life.

Daniel Ruiz wrote this **biography** about President George Washington.

biology: (biy-AHL-uh-jee) *n.* the scientific study of living things.

We studied plant life in **biology**.

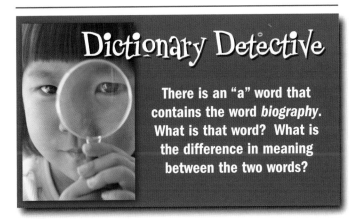

Dictionary Detective

There is an "a" word that contains the word *biography*. What is that word? What is the difference in meaning between the two words?

Bb

bird: (burd) *n.* a type of animal with feathers, wings, and a beak.

The **bird** landed on the branch.

blue: (bloo) *adj.* a color.

This is the color **blue**.

birthday: (BURTH-day) *n.* the celebration of the day a person was born.

We put candles on the cake for Lucy's **birthday**.

body: (BAHD-ee) *n.* all of the physical parts of a person or animal.

Her **body** was tired after playing in the park.

black: (blak) *adj.* a color.

This is the color **black**.

block: (blahk) *n.* a cube-shaped toy used for building.

Marcus used **blocks** to build a tower.

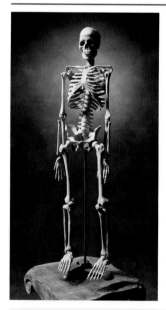

bone: (bohn) *n.* one of the many white, hard parts of a human or animal skeleton.

The human skeleton contains many **bones**.

blouse: (blows) *n.* a shirt made for women or girls.

Kristin wore this **blouse** for the class picture.

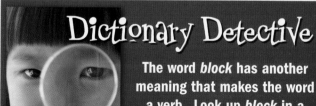

Dictionary Detective

The word *block* has another meaning that makes the word a verb. Look up *block* in a standard dictionary to find out the other meaning. Use the verb form of this word in a sentence.

book: (buk) *n.* a written work on sheets of paper bound together with a cover.

Sylvia read the **book** twice.

boot: (boot) *n.* a shoe that covers the foot and part of the leg.

These **boots** will protect your feet.

bottom: (BAHT-um) *adj.* the lowest or deepest part.

The river runs through the **bottom** of this canyon.

boundary: (BOWN-dree) *n.* border; something that shows the limits.

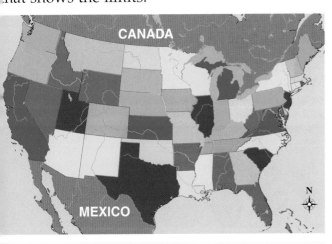

The **boundaries** of the United States separate it from Canada to the north and Mexico to the south.

bow and arrow: (boh and AYR-oh) *n.* a slender, pointed object and the machine used to shoot it.

Cindy's father showed her how to use a **bow and arrow** safely.

bowl: (bohl) *n.* a round dish used for holding liquids or food.

Darrell filled the blue **bowl** with popcorn.

boxer: (BAHK-sur) *n.* a person who fights as a sport.

The **boxer** is preparing for the boxing match.

boy: (boi) *n.* a male child.

This **boy** plays the tambourine in the band.

25

Bb

boycott: (BOI-kaht) *v.* to protest by not buying or using something.

Some people **boycotted** the store because of its very high prices.

bracelet: (BRAYS-lit) *n.* a chain or band worn on the wrist.

Stephanie wears this silver **bracelet** every day.

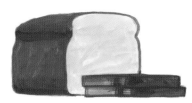

bread: (bred) *n.* a baked food made of flour, salt, yeast, and other ingredients.

We need **bread** to make sandwiches.

breakfast: (BREK-fust) *n.* the first meal of the day.

Eating a healthy **breakfast** in the morning is good for you.

bridge: (brij) *n.* a structure over a river or road.

The **bridge** allows cars to drive over the river.

broom: (broom) *n.* an object used for sweeping.

Use the **broom** to sweep the floor.

brother: (BRUHTH-ur) *n.* a male relative who has the same parents as another person.

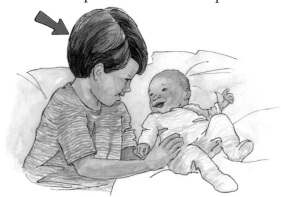

The baby's older **brother** plays with him every day.

brown: (brown) *adj.* a color.

This is the color **brown**.

brush: (bruhsh) *n.* a tool with bristles and a handle.

She used a **brush** and dustpan to clean up the dirt.

bucket: (BUHK-it) *n.* a container; a pail.

We need a **bucket** of water to mop the floor.

buffalo: (BUHF-uh-loh) *n.* a large wild mammal with horns and a hump on its back.

Many **buffalo** live in the Great Plains region of the United States.

bug: (buhg) *n.* any insect.

A **bug** crawled across the floor.

bulletin board: (BUL-uh-tun bohrd) *n.* a board for posting notices and announcements.

The new class schedule is on the **bulletin board**.

bus: (buhs) *n.* a large, long vehicle with many seats.

Angelica rides the **bus** home after work.

bus driver: (buhs DRIY-vur) *n.* a person who drives a bus.

The **bus driver** is waving to the people on the street.

bush: (bush) *n.* a low plant.

The **bush** is growing next to the wall.

27

butcher: (BUCH-ur) *n.* a person who cuts or sells meat.

Peter bought steaks from the **butcher**.

butter: (BUHT-ur) *n.* a yellowish spread used for cooking.

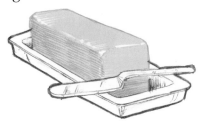

Maria likes **butter** on her bread.

butterfly: (BUHT-ur-fliy) *n.* a flying insect with antennae, a thin body, and wings.

The **butterfly** flew away over the fence.

by: (biy) *prep.* near or next to.

She stood **by** the table.

cafeteria: (kaf-uh-TEER-ee-uh) *n.* a room where food is sold and eaten.

The students eat lunch in the **cafeteria**.

cake: (kayk) *n.* a sweet, baked food, usually containing flour, sugar, and eggs.

Cake is my favorite dessert.

calculate: (KAL-kyoo-layt) *v.* to determine by using math.

She **calculated** that the sale price would be $100.

calendar: (KAL-uhn-dur) *n.* a chart with the days of each week and month in the year.

The **calendar** shows how many days are in September.

calf: (kaf) *n.* a mammal; a young cow.

The **calf** is too young to be away from its mother.

calm: (kahm) *adj.* peaceful; relaxed.

The children were **calm** as they read stories by the fire.

camel: (KAM-ul) *n.* a large, humped mammal used to carry people or goods.

People can use **camels** to cross the desert.

camper: (KAM-pur) *n.* a vehicle people can live and sleep in.

All the supplies for our trip are in the **camper**.

29

Cc

can opener: (kan OH-puhn-ur) *n.* a tool used to open cans.

She used a **can opener** to open the can of soup.

canal: (kuh-NAL) *n.* a ditch or other waterway dug into the ground to carry the flow of water.

canal

Farmers dig **canals** to bring water to their crops.

candidate: (KAN-duh-dayt) *n.* a person who wants to be elected to a position.

The **candidates** for city council each gave a speech.

canoe: (kuh-NOO) *n.* a slender boat.

Carlos rowed the **canoe** across the lake.

cape: (kayp) *n.* a point of land that extends into a sea or other body of water.

This photograph shows **Cape** St. Vincent in Portugal.

Richmond
Virginia

capital: (KAP-uh-tul) *n.* the city that is the official place of government for a state or country.

Richmond is the **capital** of Virginia.

capitalism: (KAP-i-tul-iz-um) *n.* an economic system in which individuals have the ability to create wealth.

The U.S. economy is based on **capitalism**.

car: (kahr) *n.* a common vehicle; automobile.

The **car** is parked on the street.

30

carbon dioxide: (KAHR-bun diy-AHK-siyd) *n.* a gas in the air that animals breathe out and plants take in.

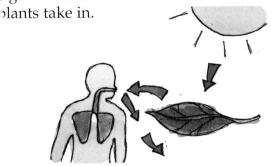

Plants take in **carbon dioxide** and release oxygen that humans and animals can breathe.

careful: (KAYR-ful) *adj.* cautious.

The girl was **careful** and made sure the water was warm.

carnivore: (KAHR-nuh-vohr) *n.* an animal that eats other animals.

Lions are **carnivores** and hunt the animals they eat.

carpenter: (KAHR-puhn-tur) *n.* a person who builds or repairs wooden structures.

The **carpenter** built a new room.

carrot: (KAYR-ut) *n.* a long, orange vegetable.

He ate a **carrot** with his lunch.

cat: (kat) *n.* a small, mammal with pointed ears and a tail.

Our **cat** is very furry and fat.

caterpillar: (KAT-ur-pil-ur) *n.* the wormlike form of a butterfly or moth.

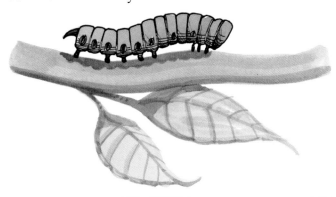

One day the **caterpillar** will become a butterfly.

CD: (SEE-DEE) *n.* a compact disc; a thin disc containing music or other data.

My favorite song is on this **CD**.

31

Cc

CD player: (SEE-DEE PLAY-ur) *n.* a machine used for playing compact discs (CDs).

I listened to music on my new **CD player**.

---

ceiling: (SEE-ling) *n.* the top surface of a room.

The light hangs from the **ceiling**.

---

celery: (SEL-ur-ee) *n.* a stiff, green vegetable.

Celery is often used in soups and salads.

---

cell: (sel) *n.* the basic part of all plants and animals.

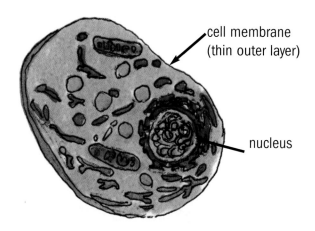

cell membrane (thin outer layer)

nucleus

All **cells** contain a nucleus and a cell membrane.

cement mixer: (si-MENT MIK-sur) *n.* a vehicle used to mix large amounts of cement.

The construction company uses a **cement mixer**.

---

center: (SEN-tur) *n.* the core or middle of something.

To begin the game, Gloria sat in the **center** of the circle.

---

century: (SEN-chu-ree) *n.* a period of 100 years.

1500 1600 1700 1800 1900 2000

The automobile was invented in the 20th **century**.

---

cereal: (SEER-ee-ul) *n.* a breakfast food made from wheat, oats, or other grains.

WHEAT

I eat **cereal** with milk for breakfast.

ceremony: (SER-uh-moh-nee) *n.* the formal activities conducted on a special occasion.

During their wedding **ceremony**, the couple gave each other rings.

chain: (chayn) *n.* a series of connected metal rings.

He used the **chain** to lock the gate.

chair: (chayr) *n.* a seat for one person.

Each student in the class sits in a **chair**.

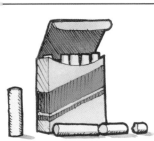

chalk: (chahk) *n.* a piece of powdery material used to write on a blackboard or other surface.

The teacher got a new box of **chalk**.

chalkboard: (CHAHK-bohrd) *n.* a blackboard.

Patrice's teacher let her write on the **chalkboard**.

change: (chaynj) *n.* coins used to buy things.

I have enough **change** to buy a soda.

character: (KAR-uhk-tur) *n.* a person in a story or play.

Candide is the main **character** in Voltaire's play *Candide*.

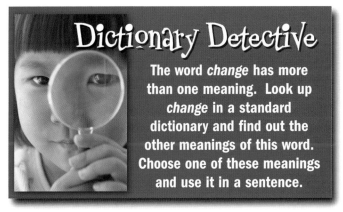

Dictionary Detective

The word *change* has more than one meaning. Look up *change* in a standard dictionary and find out the other meanings of this word. Choose one of these meanings and use it in a sentence.

Cc

characteristic: (kayr-uhk-tuh-RIS-tik) *n.* a distinctive quality of a person or thing.

The zebra's stripes are a unique **characteristic**.

cheap: (cheep) *adj.* costing very little; not valuable.

He bought a **cheap** model car for 25 cents.

check: (chek) *n.* a written document directing the bank to pay money.

John wrote a **check** to pay his phone bill.

checker: (CHEK-ur) *n.* a person who sees what you want to buy and takes your money for the items; a cashier.

I paid the **checker** for the groceries.

cheek: (cheek) *n.* the part of the body on either side of the face, below the eyes and above the jaws.

His **cheeks** got bigger when he blew out the candles.

cheese: (cheez) *n.* a food made from milk.

She likes to eat **cheese** and crackers.

chemical: (KEM-i-kul) *n.* a substance.

Scientists carefully handle the **chemicals** they study.

chemist: (KEM-ist) *n.* an expert in the science of chemistry.

The **chemist** is doing research.

cherry: (CHAYR-ee) *n.* a small round fruit with a hard seed in the center.

Susie likes a **cherry** on top of her ice cream.

chest of drawers: (chest uv drohrz) *n.* a cabinet for storing clothes or other items.

I keep my clothes in this **chest of drawers**.

chick: (chik) *n.* a young chicken.

The yellow **chick** is only a few days old.

chicken: (CHIK-un) *n.* a bird with a beak and feathers.

Chickens lay eggs almost every day.

child: (chiyld) *n.* a young person, either a girl or a boy.

The **child** is going to a new school.

chimney: (CHIM-nee) *n.* a structure that carries smoke from a fireplace.

The black smoke is coming out of the **chimney**.

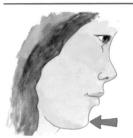

chin: (chin) *n.* the lowest part of the face, below the mouth.

The red arrow is pointing to the girl's **chin**.

chipmunk: (CHIP-munk) *n.* a small, brown mammal with a striped body and tail.

The **chipmunk** searched the ground for nuts and seeds.

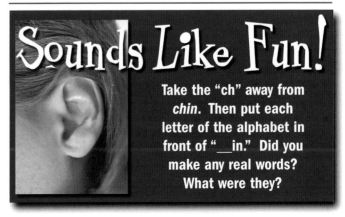

Sounds Like Fun!

Take the "ch" away from *chin*. Then put each letter of the alphabet in front of "__in." Did you make any real words? What were they?

Cc

chlorophyll: (KLOHR-uh-fil) *n.* the green substance in plants and algae.

Chlorophyll makes plants green and helps them turn light into food.

chromosome: (KROH-muh-sohm) *n.* the part of a cell that carries genes, which determine characteristics such as eye color.

The study of human **chromosomes** has taught us a lot about diseases.

circle: (SUR-kul) *n.* a round shape with all points on the edge being the same distance from the center.

The girl drew an orange **circle**.

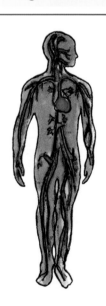

circulate: (SUR-kyoo-layt) *v.* to move through a circuit, such as blood through the body.

Blood **circulates** throughout the body.

circumference: (sur-KUHM-fur-uns) *n.* the distance around a circle.

The **circumference** of a circle can be calculated using a math equation.

citizen: (SIT-uh-zun) *n.* a member of a state or nation.

These U.S. **citizens** are pledging allegiance to the country's flag.

city: (SIT-ee) *n.* a large town.

The **city** has many tall buildings.

civil war: (SIV-uhl wohr) *n.* a war between regions or factions within the same country.

The American **Civil War** was from 1861 to 1865.

civilization: (siv-uh-li-ZAY-shun) *n.* a culture or society of a particular place or time.

You can see the remains of the Inca **civilization** in this picture.

civilized: (SIV-uh-liyzd) *adj.* to be civil, enlightened, refined, or orderly.

Human beings today are more **civilized** than the Neanderthals who lived more than 30,000 years ago.

clean: (kleen) *v.* to remove dirt.

He **cleaned** the carpet with the vacuum.

clear: (kleer) *adj.* transparent; see-through.

The lenses in these glasses are **clear**.

clever: (KLEV-ur) *adj.* intelligent; smart.

The **clever** boy solved the puzzles.

cliff: (klif) *n.* the steep, almost vertical edge of a mesa, plateau, hill, mountain, or plain.

This photograph shows a very steep **cliff**.

climate: (KLIY-mit) *n.* the temperature, rainfall, and wind conditions of a region over a period of time.

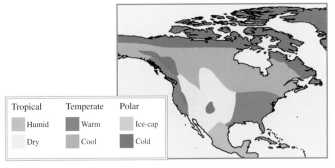

Tropical	Temperate	Polar
Humid	Warm	Ice-cap
Dry	Cool	Cold

Many people like the **climate** of the American Southwest because the summers are hot and dry.

Dictionary Detective

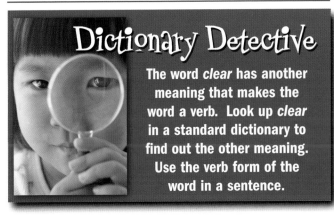

The word *clear* has another meaning that makes the word a verb. Look up *clear* in a standard dictionary to find out the other meaning. Use the verb form of the word in a sentence.

clock: (klahk) *n.* a machine that shows the time.

According to the **clock**, it is 3:30.

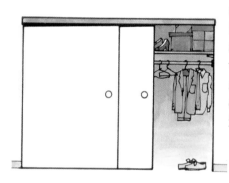

closet: (KLAHZ-it) *n.* a small cabinet where clothes, shoes, and other personal items are kept.

José hangs his clothes in the **closet**.

clothesline: (KLOHZ-liyn) *n.* a rope or cord on which clean clothes are hung to dry.

Bret hung the clothes on the **clothesline**.

clothespin: (KLOHZ-pin) *n.* a specially designed piece of wood or plastic that can be used for hanging clothes on a clothesline.

I need one more **clothespin** to finish hanging the clothes.

cloud: (klowd) *n.* a visible collection of water or ice in the air.

The **cloud** drifted in the sky.

cloudy: (KLOW-dee) *adj.* to be covered with clouds.

The sky is **cloudy** today.

clown: (klown) *n.* a funny performer with makeup and a costume who tries to make people laugh.

The **clown** entertained the children at the school's festival.

coach: (kohch) *n.* a person who trains an athlete or team.

The **coach** was proud of the team.

oast: (kohst) *n.* the land next to the ocean; eashore.

San Francisco is a large city on the western **coast** of the United States.

coat: (koht) *n.* an outer garment that covers most of the body.

A **coat** can keep you dry and warm.

coffee maker: (KAW-fee MAY-kur) *n.* a machine for brewing coffee.

She turned on the **coffee maker** in the morning.

coffeepot: (KAW-fee-paht) *n.* a container used to make or serve coffee.

She brought the **coffeepot** to the table and poured herself a cup of coffee.

cold: (kohld) *adj.* having a low temperature; lacking warmth.

The family bundled in warm clothes during the **cold** weather.

collect: (kuh-LEKT) *v.* to gather together.

Martin **collects** seashells on the beach.

colony: (KAWL-uh-nee) *n.* a group of people who form a settlement in a new land.

The Jamestown **colony** developed beside the James River.

Cc

color: (KUHL-ur) *v.* to fill in a drawing with paint, crayons, or another substance.

The girl **colored** the pictures for her school project.

colt: (kohlt) *n.* a mammal; a young male horse.

The **colt** has a white spot on its head.

comb: (kohm) *n.* something used to fix hair.

He used the **comb** to fix his hair.

comedy: (KAWM-uh-dee) *n.* any play, movie, or television show that is funny.

The **comedy** made the boy laugh.

command: (kuh-MAND) *v.* to order; to direct with authority.

The military officer **commanded** the soldiers to stand at attention.

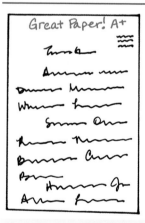

comment: (KAWM-ent) *n.* a remark.

The teacher's **comments** on my paper made me very happy.

commerce: (KAWM-urs) *n.* trade.

The U.S. Department of **Commerce** is responsible for the United States' trade with other countries.

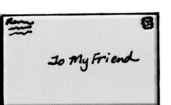

communicate: (kuh-MYOO-nuh-kayt) *v.* to express thoughts or information through writing, speaking, and so forth.

Allison and her friend like to **communicate** by writing each other letters.

communism: (KAWM-yuh-niz-um) *n.* an economic system in which all property and money is owned by the community as a whole.

Communism does not allow individual people to create wealth or own property.

community: (kuh-MYOO-nuh-tee) *n.* a group of people who live in the same area, share a government, and often have a common background.

The people in our **community** often gather in the summer for outdoor parties.

compass: (KUHM-pus) *n.* an instrument for determining directions.

According to the **compass**, we are headed north.

compete: (kuhm-PEET) *v.* to try to get or win something.

Devon and Rene **competed** in the state chess championship.

complain: (kuhm-PLAYN) *v.* to express pain, unhappiness, or dissatisfaction.

She **complained** that her head hurt.

complicated: (KAWM-pluh-kay-tid) *adj.* complex; difficult to explain.

Fixing a broken engine can be a **complicated** process.

compromise: (KAWM-pruh-miyz) *n.* an agreement made when people have different opinions.

I wanted to leave at 6:00 and Gary wanted to leave at 8:00, so we **compromised** and left at 7:00.

computer: (kuhm-PYOO-tur) *n.* a machine used for typing, storing information, and connecting to the Internet.

The students type their papers on the **computer**.

concentrate: (KAHN-suhn-trayt) *v.* to focus one's attention.

She **concentrated** on the difficult test questions.

concern: (kuhn-SURN) *n.* worry or anxiety.

The father was **concerned** about his son's high temperature.

conflict: (kun-FLIKT) *v.* to be in opposition; to clash.

MONDAY	1:00
9:00	2:00
10:00　Meeting with John	3:00
11:00	4:00　Go to Doctor
	Cindy's Soccer Game
12:00	5:00

The doctor's appointment **conflicts** with Cindy's soccer game.

confront: (kuhn-FRUNT) *v.* to oppose.

The two animals **confronted** each other.

confused: (kuhn-FYOOZD) *adj.* to be mixed up; to not understand.

The math problem **confused** him.

congratulate: (kuhn-GRACH-oo-layt) *v.* to express pleasure to another person for an accomplishment or good fortune.

The principal **congratulated** Francine on receiving a college scholarship.

connect: (kuh-NEKT) *v.* to join or unite.

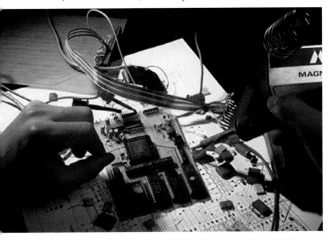

He **connected** the parts to make the computer work.

consider: (kuhn-SID-ur) *v.* to think about carefully in order to make a decision.

They will **consider** the architect's plans for the new building.

constellation: (kahn-stuh-LAY-shun) *n.* a group of stars that has been named.

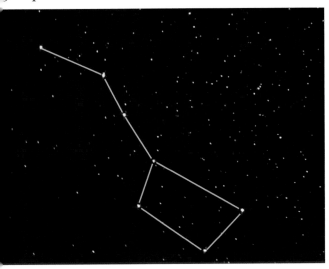

On clear evenings, you can see **constellations** such as the Big Dipper.

constitution: (kahn-stuh-TOO-shun) *n.* a system of laws that explain the role of the government and the rights of the people in the nation.

The U.S. **Constitution** established a system of laws.

construct: (kuhn-STRUHKT) *v.* to build.

They are working together to **construct** a house.

container: (kuhn-TAY-nur) *n.* an object such as a box, carton, or can that can hold something.

The children put their toys in this **container**.

contemporary: (kuhn-TEM-puh-rayr-ee) *n.* belonging to the same period of time.

Writers Langston Hughes and Zora Neale Hurston were **contemporaries**.

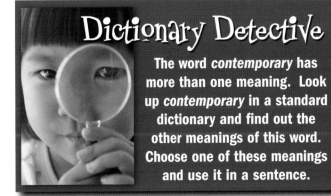

Dictionary Detective

The word *contemporary* has more than one meaning. Look up *contemporary* in a standard dictionary and find out the other meanings of this word. Choose one of these meanings and use it in a sentence.

43

Cc

continent: (KAHN-tuh-nunt) *n.* one of the main landmasses of the earth.

Africa is the second largest **continent**.

control: (kuhn-TROHL) *v.* to have power over something or someone.

The firefighters are trying to **control** the fire.

convince: (kuhn-VINS) *v.* to persuade.

He **convinced** them to buy the car by showing them all the safety features.

cook: (kuk) *n.* a person who prepares food.

The **cook** made pancakes.

cookie: (KUK-ee) *n.* a small, flat cakelike food.

My favorite kind of **cookie** is chocolate chip.

corn: (kohrn) *n.* a plant with kernels that is used for food.

He likes to eat **corn** on the cob.

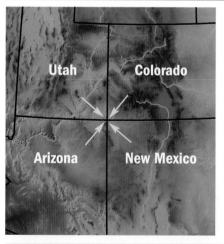

corner: (KOHR-nur) *n.* the place where two lines or surfaces meet.

The place where the states of Arizona, Colorado, New Mexico, and Utah meet is called "four **corners**."

cottage cheese: (KAHT-ij cheez) *n.* a soft, loose cheese made from milk.

She eats **cottage cheese** in the afternoon.

44

count: (kownt) *v.* to figure out how many things or people there are.

We **counted** five cows.

country: (KUHN-tree) *n.* a nation.

ITALY

Italy is a **country** on the continent of Europe.

courage: (KUR-ij) *n.* bravery.

It took **courage** for Dr. Martin Luther King, Jr. to speak out against injustice.

courteous: (KUR-tee-us) *adj.* showing good manners; polite.

In Japan, it is **courteous** for people to greet each other with a bow.

cousin: (KUZ-un) *n.* the son or daughter of an uncle or aunt.

Her **cousin** comes to visit every summer.

cow: (kow) *n.* a large female mammal that has horns and produces milk.

The farmer milks the **cow** every day.

cowboy: (KOW-boi) *n.* a man who watches over and herds cattle.

The **cowboy** spent all day looking for the lost calf.

cowgirl: (KOW-gurl) *n.* a woman who watches over and herds cattle.

The **cowgirl** works on a ranch.

Cc

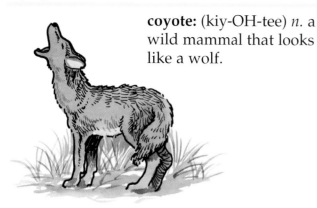

coyote: (kiy-OH-tee) *n.* a wild mammal that looks like a wolf.

The **coyote** howls at the moon.

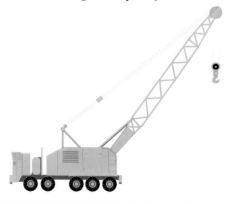

cracker: (KRAK-ur) *n.* a thin, crisp biscuit.

I like to eat soup with **crackers**.

crane: (krayn) *n.* a vehicle with a machine for lifting and moving heavy objects.

They used a **crane** to move the cement blocks.

crayon: (KRAY-awn) *n.* a colored stick used for coloring or drawing.

Mei used a pink **crayon** to draw flowers.

crib: (krib) *n.* a baby's bed with enclosed sides.

The baby sleeps in a **crib**.

critical: (KRIT-i-kul) *adj.* inclined to find fault.

Reviewers were **critical** of the movie and told people not to see it.

criticize: (KRIT-uh-siyz) *v.* to find fault with.

The art teacher **criticized** the painting.

crop: (krahp) *n.* a plant grown for food.

The rain helped the **crops** grow.

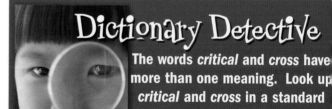

Dictionary Detective

The words *critical* and *cross* have more than one meaning. Look up *critical* and *cross* in a standard dictionary and find out the other meanings of these words. Choose one of these meanings and use it in a sentence.

46

crowd: (krowd) *n.* a large group of people.

A **crowd** gathered to watch the football game.

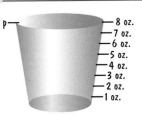

culture: (KUHL-chur) *n.* the lifestyle, ideas, and traditions of a group of people.

Cinco de Mayo is an important holiday in Mexican **culture**.

cup: (kuhp) *n.* a unit of eight fluid ounces.

This recipe calls for one **cup** of milk.

cup and saucer: (kup and SAW-sur) *n.* a container with a handle for drinking hot liquids and the shallow dish that holds it.

We need another **cup and saucer** for the tea party.

cupcake: (KUHP-kayk) *n.* a small cake for one person.

I ate a **cupcake** at the party.

curious: (KYOOR-ee-us) *adj.* eager to know; inquisitive.

The **curious** cat looked outside the window.

currency: (KUR-uhn-see) *n.* any form of money.

The dollar is the basic unit of U.S. **currency**.

current: (KUR-unt) *n.* the movement of an electric charge through a wire.

The **current** is coming from the electrical outlet.

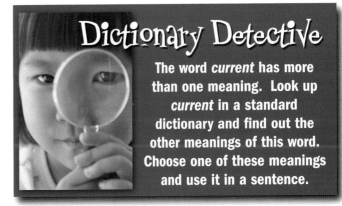

Dictionary Detective

The word *current* has more than one meaning. Look up *current* in a standard dictionary and find out the other meanings of this word. Choose one of these meanings and use it in a sentence.

47

curve: (kurv) *n.* the shape created by a bending line.

There's a **curve** in the road up ahead.

custodian: (kuhs-TOH-dee-un) *n.* a person at a school or other building who cleans and does repairs; janitor.

The **custodian** keeps our school clean.

custom: (KUHS-tum) *n.* a regular practice; tradition.

It is a **custom** in the United States to eat turkey on Thanksgiving.

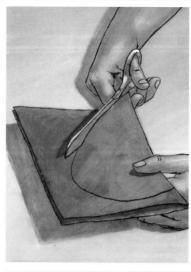

cut: (kuht) *v.* to separate with a sharp-edged instrument.

She used the scissors to **cut** the paper.

daily: (DAY-lee) *adj.* occurring each day.

He reads the **daily** newspaper before going to work.

damage: (DAM-ij) *n.* injury or harm.

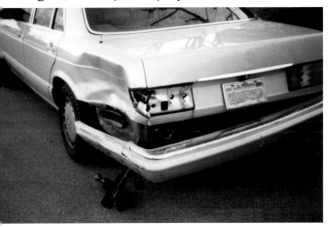

The accident caused **damage** to the car.

dancer: (DANS-ur) *n.* a person who dances.

The **dancer** is graceful when she jumps.

data: (DAY-tuh) *n.* information.

Computers today can hold a large amount of **data**.

Money Earned	$10,000
Money Spent	$15,000
Debt	$ 5,000

debt: (det) *n.* something, particularly money, that is owed.

He is in **debt** because he spent more money than he earned.

decade: (DEK-ayd) *n.* a period of 10 years.

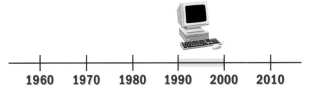

| 1960 | 1970 | 1980 | 1990 | 2000 | 2010 |

The Internet became very popular during the **decade** of the 1990s.

decay: (di-KAY) *v.* to rot.

decay

If you do not take care of your teeth, they may **decay**.

deceive: (di-SEEV) *v.* to trick someone into believing something is true.

I was **deceived** by the boy wearing the mask.

December: (di-SEM-bur) *n.* the twelfth month of the year.

Many schools take a winter break in **December**.

49

Dd

decision: (di-SIZH-un) *n.* the act of making up one's mind.

The townspeople gathered to hear the **decision**.

declare: (di-KLAYR) *v.* to announce formally; to state or say officially.

The mayor **declared** a holiday to honor the town's hero.

deep: (deep) *adj.* extending far down.

Lisa dove into the **deep** end of the pool.

deer: (deer) *n.* a mammal with long legs and antlers that lives in wooded areas.

The **deer** stopped suddenly.

defend: (di-FEND) *v.* to protect; to guard against injury.

The lawyer **defended** the man who was accused of a crime.

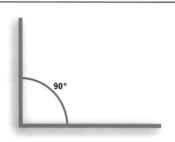

degree: (di-GREE) *n.* a unit of measure; the 360 parts of a full circle

This angle is 90 **degrees**.

delicious: (di-LISH-us) *adj.* pleasing to the sense of taste and smell.

These pancakes are **delicious**.

deliver: (di-LIV-ur) *v.* to bring an item, such as a package or letter, to the person for whom it was intended.

The postal carrier **delivers** mail to our house.

democracy: (di-MAHK-ruh-see) *n.* a form of government in which the people, or the officials elected by the people, hold the power.

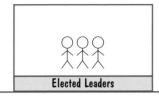

Elected Leaders

People

In a **democracy**, people elect their representatives.

den: (den) *n.* a room in a home for informal activities like reading and games.

We played games and watched TV in the **den**.

dentist: (DEN-tist) *n.* a person whose job it is to treat the teeth and gums.

The **dentist** said I don't have any tooth decay.

depend: (di-PEND) *v.* to rely on.

Mr. Jones **depends** on the bus to get to work.

depression: (di-PRESH-un) *n.* a period in which business suffers and many people don't have jobs.

UNEMPLOYMENT—1925–1945

During the Great **Depression**, many Americans lost their jobs.

desert: (DEZ-urt) *n.* a dry, sandy region that gets very little water.

Cactus plants grow in the **desert**.

design: (di-ZIYN) *v.* to plan or sketch something that will be built.

A man in England **designed** the first cotton spinning machine.

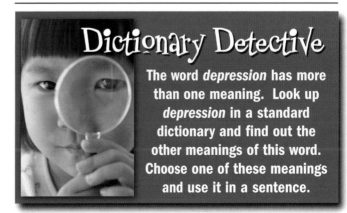

Dictionary Detective

The word *depression* has more than one meaning. Look up *depression* in a standard dictionary and find out the other meanings of this word. Choose one of these meanings and use it in a sentence.

Dd

designate: (DEZ-ig-nayt) *v.* to select someone to do something.

Lance was **designated** to read our group report to the class.

desk: (desk) *n.* a piece of furniture with a surface for writing and drawers for papers and other items.

The teacher graded papers at her **desk**.

desperate: (DES-pur-it) *adj.* having an urgent need.

The lost traveler was **desperate** for water.

destroy: (di-STROI) *v.* to ruin or spoil; to wreck.

The fire **destroyed** thousands of acres of land.

diagonal: (diy-AG-uh-nul) *adj.* sloping or slanting

He drew a **diagonal** line across the page.

School Play

Sara: [walking toward Joe] Hi Joe! How was school today?

Joe: [smiling at Sara] School was great! We spent a lot of time doing algebra, which is my favorite subject!

Sara: Really? Algebra is my favorite subject, too!

dialogue: (DIY-uh-log) *n.* conversation between two or more people.

The students learned the **dialogue** for the school play.

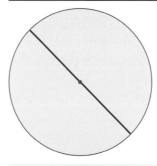

diameter: (diy-AM-uh-tur) *n.* a straight line passing through the center of a circle and meeting the surface of the circle at each end.

You can solve many math problems if you know the **diameter** of a circle.

diamond: (DIY-mund) *n.* a shape with four sides and pointed corners.

She drew a blue **diamond** on her paper.

diaper: (DIY-pur) *n.* underpants worn by a baby not yet toilet-trained.

The mother changes the baby's **diaper** several times a day.

diary: (DIY-uh-ree) *n.* a daily written record of one's experiences.

Louisa writes in her **diary** every night.

dictatorship: (dik-TAY-tur-ship) *n.* a form of government in which one person has all the power without the support of the people.

Many Roman senators thought Julius Caesar would turn Rome's republic into a **dictatorship**.

difference: (DIF-ur-uns) *n.* the amount left over when subtracting one number from another.

When you subtract 15 from 25, the **difference** is 10.

different: (DIF-uh-rent) *adj.* not alike; dissimilar.

Lupe and Erin have **different** hair styles.

difficult: (DIF-i-kult) *adj.* requiring effort or skill; hard.

Riding a bike up a hill is **difficult**.

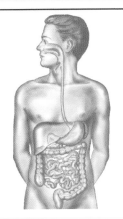

digestion: (diy-JES-chun) *n.* the process by which food is broken down and absorbed into the body.

We studied **digestion** in health class.

digit: (DIJ-it) *n.* 1. any of the Arabic numerals (0, 1, 2, 3, 4, 5, 6, 7, 8, 9). 2. a human finger or toe.

01234 56789

1. The last **digit** in this series of numbers is nine.

2. My thumb is the shortest **digit** on my hand.

dime: (diym) *n.* a U.S. coin worth 10 cents.

I had two **dimes** in my pocket.

dining room: (DIYN-ing room) *n.* a room in which meals are eaten.

We eat dinner in the **dining room**.

dinner: (DIN-ur) *n.* the main meal of the day.

We had steak and salad for **dinner**.

dinosaur: (DIY-nuh-sohr) *n.* a reptile that is now extinct.

Dinosaurs lived millions of years ago.

dirty: (DUR-tee) *adj.* soiled with dirt; unclean.

After playing outside, she was completely **dirty**.

disappear: (dis-uh-PEER) *v.* to vanish from sight.

The magician made it seem as if the woman's body **disappeared**.

disappoint: (dis-uh-POINT) *v.* to not get something you hoped for.

She was **disappointed** when her friend didn't come to the party.

discover: (dis-KUV-ur) *v.* to find something previously unknown.

We sometimes say Christopher Columbus **discovered** America, even though people were living there long before his arrival.

Dd

disease: (di-ZEEZ) *n.* illness; sickness.

A terrible **disease** spread through Europe in the 1300s.

dish: (dish) *n.* an open, shallow container for holding or serving food.

Hiroko put her food on the **dish**.

dishpan: (DISH-pan) *n.* a flat-bottomed container for washing dishes.

The woman placed her dirty dishes in the **dishpan**.

diskette: (dis-KET) *n.* a floppy disk; a disk that holds computer data.

She saved her essay on a **diskette**.

dispute: (dis-PYOOT) *n.* an argument or debate.

The student explained the **dispute** about one of Isaac Newton's ideas.

dissolve: (di-ZOLV) *v.* to melt; to become liquid.

Sugar **dissolves** in hot tea.

distort: (dis-TOHRT) *v.* to twist out of shape.

Her reflection was **distorted** in the carnival mirror.

distract: (dis-TRAKT) *v.* to draw one's attention away from something.

The fly **distracted** him from his studies.

55

Dd

disturb: (dis-TURB) *v.* to interrupt or bother.

The tired travelers did not want to be **disturbed**.

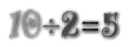

division: (di-VIZH-un) *n.* the process of figuring out how many times one number fits into another number.

Using **division**, we know that 10 divided by two equals five.

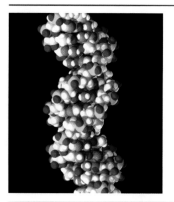

DNA: (DEE EN AY) *n.* deoxyribonucleic acid; the main component of the chromosome, the part of the cell that determines people's characteristics.

By comparing **DNA**, scientists can tell if two people are related.

doctor: (DAHK-tur) *n.* a person trained to help people who are hurt or sick.

The **doctor** said Connie is healthy.

dog: (dawg) *n.* a four-legged mammal related to a wolf; dogs come in different shapes and sizes.

He takes the **dog** for a walk every night.

doll: (dahl) *n.* a small toy that looks like a person.

The little girl carries this **doll** everywhere she goes.

dollar bill: (DAHL-ur bil) *n.* a piece of paper indicating one unit of U.S. currency; equal to 100 cents.

I used a **dollar bill** to buy a candy bar.

dollhouse: (DAHL-hows) *n.* a small house used for playing with dolls.

She put tiny furniture in the rooms of the **dollhouse**.

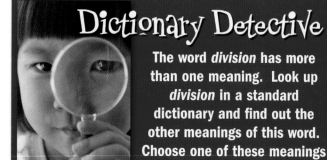

Dictionary Detective

The word *division* has more than one meaning. Look up *division* in a standard dictionary and find out the other meanings of this word. Choose one of these meanings and use it in a sentence.

dolphin: (DAHL-fin) *n.* a mammal with a pointed snout (nose and mouth) that lives in the ocean.

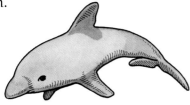

A **dolphin** swam alongside our boat.

donate: (DOH-nayt) *v.* to give; to contribute as a gift.

Mrs. Wang **donated** money to the hospital.

door: (dohr) *n.* something that people open and close to get in and out of a room or a building.

He closed the **door** when he left the room.

dot: (daht) *n.* a small, round mark.

I used my orange marker to make a **dot** on the paper.

doughnut: (DOH-nut) *n.* a small, often ring-shaped cake that is sweet to eat.

My mom buys **doughnuts** for breakfast on special occasions.

down: (down) *prep.* moving from a higher position to a lower position.

He came **down** the slide.

dozen: (DUZ-un) *n.* a group of 12.

We picked a **dozen** apples from the apple tree.

drama: (DRAH-muh) *n.* a play or other performance in which the story contains a problem.

William Shakespeare wrote many **dramas** about people and the problems they faced.

Dd

draw: (draw) *v.* to make a picture using a pen, pencil, or other writing tool; to sketch.

Keith likes to **draw** pictures of people.

dress: (dres) *n.* a garment for women or girls consisting of a top and a skirt.

She wore this purple **dress** to the party.

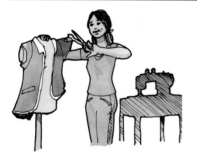

dressmaker: (DRES-may-kur) *n.* a person who makes women's clothing.

Li became a **dressmaker** because she likes to sew.

drinking fountain: (DRINK-ing FOWN-tun) *n.* a fountain from which people can drink water.

The students stopped at the **drinking fountain** after class.

drive: (driyv) *v.* to guide the movement of a vehicle.

Marcia **drives** her car to work.

drought: (drowt) *n.* a long period of dry weather.

The **drought** caused the river to dry up.

drum: (druhm) *n.* a musical instrument.

The **drum** sets the beat for the entire band.

dry: (driy) *adj.* not wet.

The weather in the desert is **dry** and hot.

duck: (duhk) *n.* a bird with webbed feet and beak.

The **duck** swam around the pond.

dune: (doon) *n.* a sand hill or ridge formed by the wind.

The windstorm created huge sand **dunes**.

during: (DYOOR-ing) *prep.* at some time in the course of.

It is not polite to talk loudly **during** a movie.

dustpan: (DUHST-pan) *n.* a short-handled shovel used to collect dust or dirt.

He used a **dustpan** and broom to remove the dirt from the patio.

DVD player: (DEE VEE DEE PLAY-ur) *n.* a machine that plays digital recordings, such as DVD movies.

We used the **DVD player** to watch the movie.

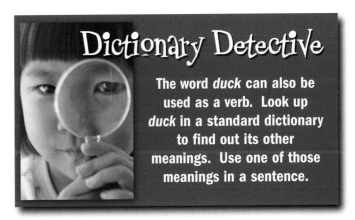

Dictionary Detective

The word *duck* can also be used as a verb. Look up *duck* in a standard dictionary to find out its other meanings. Use one of those meanings in a sentence.

Ee

eagle: (EE-gul) *n.* a bird with broad wings, a beak, and large claws.

The bald **eagle** is a symbol of the United States.

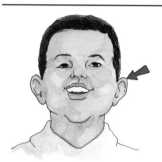

ear: (eer) *n.* the part of the body that allows you to hear.

His **ears** hurt after listening to the loud music.

earth: (urth) *n.* the third planet from the sun.

The **earth** contains seven continents and four oceans.

earthquake: (URTH-kwayk) *n.* movements on the earth's surface that are caused by volcanoes or shifts in large pieces of the earth's crust (called "tectonic plates").

Earthquakes can cause a lot of damage to buildings and homes.

east: (eest) *n.* the direction opposite of west.

On most maps, **east** is to the right.

easy: (EE-zee) *adj.* requiring little effort; not hard.

The bike ride down the hill is **easy**.

eclipse: (i-KLIPS) *n.* the event caused when the light from a star or other heavenly body is blocked.

A solar **eclipse** happens when the moon blocks the light of the sun from reaching the earth.

ecology: (i-KAHL-uh-jee) *n.* the study of the relationship between organisms and their environment.

In **ecology** class we learned how the sun helps plants and how plants help animals.

economy: (i-KON-uh-mee) *n.* the management of resources, such as money, of a country or community.

The U.S. **economy** is based on capitalism.

egg: (eg) *n.* an oval-shaped object produced by a chicken or other bird, sometimes eaten as food and sometimes hatched as a baby bird.

We found this **egg** on the chicken farm.

eight: (ayt) *n.* a number equaling seven plus one; numbers are usually used as adjectives in a sentence.

He saved **eight** pennies.

eighteen: (ay-TEEN) *n.* a number equaling 10 plus eight; numbers are usually used as adjectives in a sentence.

18

We counted **eighteen** snails in the garden.

eighth: (ayth) *adj.* the next after seventh.

The **eighth** owl landed on the tree branch.

80

eighty: (AY-tee) *n.* a number equaling 10 times eight; numbers are usually used as adjectives in a sentence.

Ten rows of eight dots make a total of **eighty** dots.

elbow: (EL-boh) *n.* the bend or joint of the human arm between the upper arm and the forearm.

It can be quite painful to bang your **elbow**.

election: (i-LEK-shun) *n.* a public vote to choose government leaders.

In the United States, we have a presidential **election** every four years.

Ee

electrician: (i-lek-TRISH-un) *n.* a person who installs or maintains electrical wiring.

The **electrician** replaced the old wiring.

electricity: (i-lek-TRIS-uh-tee) *n.* electric current or power.

The **electricity** in our house went out during the lightning storm.

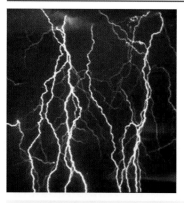

elephant: (EL-uh-funt) *n.* a very large mammal with a long trunk (nose) and tusks (teeth).

They saw the **elephant** on their trip to Africa.

22,834 feet

elevation: (el-uh-VAY-shun) *n.* the height of a mountain and other natural features.

One of the tallest peaks in the Andes Mountains reaches an **elevation** of 22,834 feet.

elevator: (EL-uh-vay-tur) *n.* a moving platform for carrying people or things from one level to another.

We took the **elevator** to the sixteenth floor.

11

eleven: (i-LEV-un) *n.* a number equaling 10 plus one; numbers are usually used as adjectives in a sentence.

We counted **eleven** caterpillars.

e-mail: (EE-mayl) *n.* a letter sent over the computer.

Josh sent an **e-mail** to his friend Maria.

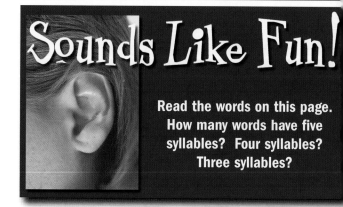

encourage: (en-KUR-ij) *v.* to inspire; to support.

The fitness trainer **encouraged** Mark to keep exercising.

Sounds Like Fun!

Read the words on this page. How many words have five syllables? Four syllables? Three syllables?

Ee

energy: (EN-ur-jee) *n.* a source of usable power.

The stove would not work without the **energy** of natural gas.

engineer: (en-juh-NEER) *n.* a person who uses science and mathematics in design and construction.

The **engineer** designed a plan for the new bridge.

enormous: (ee-NOHR-mus) *adj.* huge.

A person is **enormous** compared to an insect.

environment: (en-VIY-ruhn-munt) *n.* air, water, land, and other external factors.

The smoke polluted the **environment**.

epic: (EP-ik) *n.* a long written story about a hero who achieves great things.

The *Aeneid* by Virgil is a famous Roman **epic** written more than 2,000 years ago.

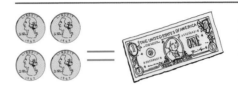

equal: (EE-kwul) *v.* to be the same as.

Four quarters are **equal** to a one dollar bill.

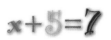

equation: (i-KWAY-zhun) *n.* a mathematical statement that uses an equal sign to show that two quantities are equal.

In the **equation** above, x = 2.

equator: (i-KWAY-tur) *n.* an imaginary circle that goes around the middle of the earth and is measured at 0 degrees.

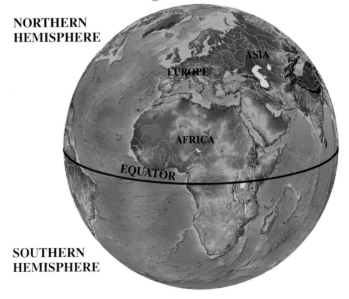

NORTHERN HEMISPHERE

EUROPE

ASIA

AFRICA

EQUATOR

SOUTHERN HEMISPHERE

If you look on a map, you'll find that Asia is located north of the **equator**.

Ee

eraser: (i-RAY-sur) *n.* a piece of rubber used to take away pencil marks.

I used the **eraser** to change my answer.

erosion: (i-ROH-zhun) *n.* when a substance slowly disappears due to water or wind.

This picture shows soil **erosion**.

erupt: (i-RUPT) *v.* to burst with force.

Hot rocks **erupted** from the volcano.

essay: (e-SAY) *n.* a written composition on a particular topic.

She wrote her **essay** on the causes of the French Revolution.

establish: (e-STAB-lish) *v.* to start up or begin.

The Pilgrims **established** a colony at Plymouth.

estimate: (ES-tuh-mayt) *v.* to make an educated guess about the amount, size, or weight of something.

The mechanic **estimated** that the repairs would cost $300.

evaporate: (i-VAP-uh-rayt) *v.* to change from a liquid into a gas.

The water in the glass **evaporated**.

evidence: (EV-uh-duns) *n.* something that supports a particular belief; proof.

The archaeologist found **evidence** that people in the past used bones to make tools.

examination: (eg-zam-uh-NAY-shun) *n.* inspection; a close look.

The doctor's **examination** of the x-rays took several minutes.

excited: (ek-SIY-tid) *adj.* very happy; stirred up to activity.

The dog is **excited** to take a walk.

exhaust: (eg-ZAWST) *n.* the gases that escape from an engine.

The **exhaust** from the train went into the air.

expand: (ek-SPAND) *v.* to increase in size.

The balloon **expands** as Chrissy blows into it.

expedition: (ek-spuh-DISH-un) *n.* a journey made for a specific purpose.

Sacagawea helped the Lewis and Clark **expedition** reach the Northwest Coast.

expenditure: (ek-SPEN-duh-chur) *n.* a charge for goods or services.

Our monthly **expenditures** include gas, electricity, and a car payment.

expensive: (ek-SPEN-siv) *adj.* costing a high price.

This diamond ring is too **expensive** for me to buy.

experience: (ek-SPEER-ee-uns) *n.* something one has personally lived through.

Visiting the White House was a memorable **experience** for the students.

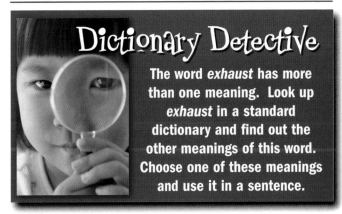

Dictionary Detective

The word *exhaust* has more than one meaning. Look up *exhaust* in a standard dictionary and find out the other meanings of this word. Choose one of these meanings and use it in a sentence.

65

Ee

experiment: (ek-SPER-uh-munt) *n.* a test to discover something unknown.

The scientist is conducting an **experiment** to see what will happen when he mixes two chemicals together.

exploration: (ek-spluh-RAY-shun) *n.* an act of investigating unknown areas.

A compass is very useful during **exploration**.

explore: (ek-SPLOHR) *v.* to travel for the purpose of discovery.

Astronauts **explore** space.

export: (ek-SPOHRT) *v.* to sell goods to other countries or places.

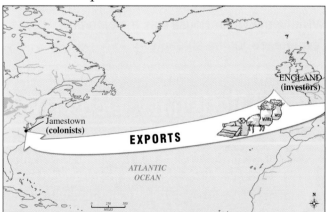

In the 1600s, England **exported** woolen coats and blankets to the American colonies.

extinct: (ek-STINGKT) *adj.* no longer in existence, no longer living.

Dinosaurs are now **extinct**.

eye: (iy) *n.* the part of the body that allows you to see.

Emily has big brown **eyes**.

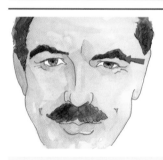

eyebrow: (IY-brow) *n.* the arch of hairs over the eye.

Vincent has thick brown **eyebrows**.

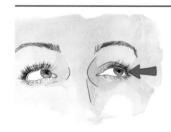

eyelash: (IY-lash) *n.* a short hair growing along the edge of the eyelid.

Some women darken their **eyelashes** with makeup.

eyelid: (IY-lid) *n.* the movable skin that covers the eyeball.

You cannot see anything when your **eyelids** are closed.

fable: (FAY-bul) *n.* a story that is not true and teaches a lesson.

In the **fable** *Beowulf*, a man kills a monster.

face: (fays) *n.* the front part of the head.

Emmanuel has a smile on his **face**.

fall: (fawl) *n.* autumn; the season between summer and winter.

In many parts of the world, the leaves change colors in the **fall**.

family: (FAM-uh-lee) *n.* a group of people closely related, such as parents and their children.

My parents, my brother, and I are a **family**.

family room: (FAM-uh-lee room) *n.* a room in a house used as the center of family activity.

We watch television together in the **family room**.

fan: (fan) *n.* a device for moving air.

The **fan** helps make the room cooler on a hot day.

fantasy: (FAN-tuh-see) *n.* something imagined and not real.

André had a **fantasy** that he was flying on a carpet.

far: (fahr) *adj.* at a great distance.

Arthur is **far** away.

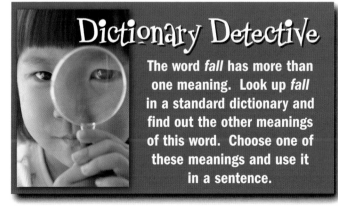

Dictionary Detective

The word *fall* has more than one meaning. Look up *fall* in a standard dictionary and find out the other meanings of this word. Choose one of these meanings and use it in a sentence.

Ff

farmer: (FAHR-mur) *n.* a person who raises food crops and animals.

The **farmer** is feeding the pig.

fast: (fast) *adj.* moving quickly.

The cheetah is a **fast** runner.

thin → fat

fat: (fat) *adj.* plump; heavy.

The cat ate so much that he became **fat**.

father: (FAH-thur) *n.* a male parent.

Jake's **father** reads him a story each night.

68

fawn: (fawn) *n.* a mammal; a young deer.

The **fawn** is standing in the stream.

February: (FEB-roo-ayr-ee) *n.* the second month of the year.

Valentine's Day is in **February**.

fertile: (FURT-ul) *adj.* able to produce a lot of something.

The apples grew on the **fertile** tree.

feudalism: (FYOOD-uhl-iz-um) *n.* an economic, political, and social system in which landowners give workers protection and use of land in exchange for their labor.

Under **feudalism**, peasants gave part of their crops to the owner of the land.

few: (fyoo) *adj.* a small amount.

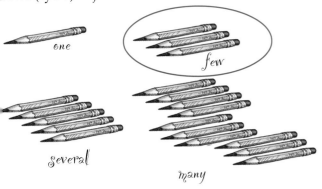

one
few
several
many

Please bring a **few** pencils with you to class.

fiction: (FIK-shun) *n.* a work of literature that is a made-up story.

The Adventures of Tom Sawyer by Mark Twain is an example of American **fiction**.

fifteen: (fif-TEEN) *n.* a number equaling 10 plus five; numbers are usually used as adjectives in a sentence.

15

We counted **fifteen** ladybugs in the bush.

fifth: (fifth) *adj.* the next after fourth.

The **fifth** owl landed on the tree branch.

fifty: (FIF-tee) *n.* a number equaling 10 times five; numbers are usually used as adjectives in a sentence.

50

Ten rows of five dots make a total of **fifty** dots.

finger: (FING-gur) *n.* one of the digits of the hand.

Steven pointed to the board with his **finger**.

fingernail: (FING-gur-nayl) *n.* the hard covering at the end of the finger.

Gloria painted her long **fingernails** pink.

finish: (FIN-ish) *v.* to complete.

Derek **finished** the race in first place.

69

Ff

fire engine: (fiyr EN-jun) *n.* a vehicle used for putting out fires.

The **fire engine** raced to the scene of the fire.

firefighter: (FIYR-fiy-tur) *n.* a person whose job it is to put out fires.

The **firefighter** helped a man escape from the burning building.

first: (furst) *adj.* being before all others in order.

The **first** owl landed on the tree branch.

fish: (fish) *n.* a type of animal with gills, fins, and scales that lives in the water.

The blue **fish** swam in the river.

five: (fiyv) *n.* a number equaling four plus one; numbers are usually used as adjectives in a sentence.

He put **five** blocks on the floor.

flag: (flag) *n.* a piece of cloth marked with a design and used as a symbol of a nation or other organization.

The **flag** of the United States has 13 stripes and 50 stars.

flight: (fliyt) *n.* the act of flying.

Melissa enjoyed her **flight** on the hang glider.

float: (floht) *v.* to remain on the surface of a liquid.

Tyler likes to **float** in the pool in an innertube.

flood: (fluhd) *n.* an overflowing of water.

The **flood** caused a lot of damage to the homes in the town.

floor: (flohr) *n.* the bottom surface of a room.

The tile **floor** is slippery when it is wet.

flower: (FLOW-ur) *n.* the blossom of a plant.

I picked this beautiful, red **flower** from the garden.

fly: (fliy) *n.* a two-winged insect.

The **fly** landed on the table.

fold: (fohld) *v.* to bend over onto itself.

Mike **folds** the clean clothes before putting them away.

folk tale: (fohk tayl) *n.* a story that may or may not be true; folk tales are usually passed down from generation to generation by a specific group of people.

The **folk tale** of Mulan tells how a young woman saved her country.

foolish: (FOOL-ish) *adj.* showing a lack of sense; unwise.

It is **foolish** to run into the street.

foot: (fut) *n.* 1. a unit of length equaling 12 inches. 2. the part of the body below the ankle, on which the body stands.

1. Most rulers are a **foot** long.

2. He put one **foot** in the water to see if it was cold.

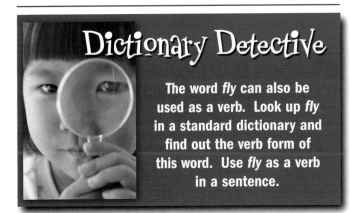

Dictionary Detective

The word *fly* can also be used as a verb. Look up *fly* in a standard dictionary and find out the verb form of this word. Use *fly* as a verb in a sentence.

Ff

football: (FUT-bawl) *n.* an oval-shaped ball used to play a sport in which two teams try to get the ball across a certain line.

Bob threw the **football** across the field.

for: (fohr) *prep.* intended to belong to someone.

This valentine is **for** Toshi.

forehead: (FOHR-id) *n.* the part of the face above the eyebrows.

When Enrique pushes his hair back, you can see his **forehead**.

foreign: (FOHR-in) *adj.* related to another country.

Gabe wants to travel to a **foreign** country.

forest: (FOHR-ist) *n.* a large area of land covered with trees and thick brush.

During the Middle Ages, people in Europe cut down many **forests** so they could plant crops on the land.

fork: (fohrk) *n.* a tool for picking up food.

You will need a **fork** to eat the ham.

formula: (FOHR-myuh-luh) *n.* a mathematical principle.

$$a^2 + b^2 = c^2$$

This is the **formula** for calculating the longest side of a right triangle.

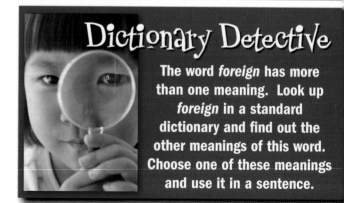

Dictionary Detective

The word *foreign* has more than one meaning. Look up *foreign* in a standard dictionary and find out the other meanings of this word. Choose one of these meanings and use it in a sentence.

fortify: (FOHR-tuh-fiy) *v.* to increase the defenses or strength of.

The king **fortified** his castle by building a wall around it.

forty: (FOHR-tee) *n.* a number equaling 10 times four; numbers are usually used as adjectives in a sentence.

40

Eight rows of five dots make a total of **forty** dots.

forward: (FOHR-wurd) *adj.* toward what is in front.

He moved **forward** to get a closer look at the painting.

fossil: (FAHS-ul) *n.* the preserved remains of a living organism.

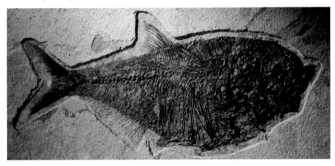

This is a **fossil** of a fish.

four: (fohr) *n.* a number equaling three plus one; numbers are usually used as adjectives in a sentence.

Four balloons floated through the air.

14 **fourteen:** (fohr-TEEN) *n.* a number equaling 10 plus four; numbers are usually used as adjectives in a sentence.

Fourteen spiders crawled across the floor.

fourth: (fohrth) *adj.* the next after third.

The **fourth** owl landed on the tree branch.

fox: (fahks) *n.* a small mammal related to the dog that has a pointed nose and a long, bushy tail.

The **fox** hid from the hunters.

fraction: (FRAK-shun) *n.* a part of a whole.

If you add these two **fractions** together, you will get a whole number.

freedom: (FREE-dum) *n.* the right to do what you want.

America's founders wrote their ideas about **freedom** in the Declaration of Independence.

freeze: (freez) *v.* the point at which water becomes a solid.

When water gets very cold, it will **freeze**.

Friday: (FRIY-day) *n.* the day of the week after Thursday and before Saturday.

Friday is our last day of school before the weekend.

friendly: (FREND-lee) *adj.* kind; nice.

The students were **friendly** with each other.

frightened: (FRIYT-und) *adj.* scared; afraid.

The boy was **frightened** when he got lost in the store.

frog: (frawg) *n.* an amphibian that hops and has smooth, moist skin.

The **frog** hopped into the pond.

from: (fruhm) *prep.* the source of something.

This gift is **from** Marco.

frying pan: (FRIY-ing pan) *n.* a shallow, long-handled pan used for cooking.

She made scrambled eggs in the **frying pan**.

fuel: (FYOO-ul) *n.* something used to produce heat or power; gasoline, kerosene, and propane are different kinds of fuel.

Kerosene is the kind of **fuel** that makes this lamp work.

fungus: (FUHNG-us) *n.* organisms such as mushrooms, molds, mildews, and yeasts.

This mushroom is a type of **fungus**.

funny: (FUHN-ee) *adj.* humorous; comical; amusing.

Kristin thought the story was very **funny**.

future: (FYOO-chur) *n.* time that is to come.

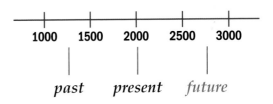

We can only guess what events may happen in the **future**.

Gg

gallon: (GAL-un) *n.* a unit of measurement equal to four quarts.

I bought a **gallon** of milk at the store.

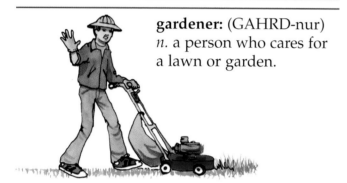

game: (gaym) *n.* a fun activity.

Let's play a **game** after we finish our homework.

gardener: (GAHRD-nur) *n.* a person who cares for a lawn or garden.

The **gardener** trimmed the grass.

gas: (gas) *n.* a substance like helium or oxygen; not solid or liquid.

The **gas** floated through the air.

gasoline: (GAS-uh-leen) *n.* a liquid used for fuel in automobiles.

Most cars cannot run without **gasoline**.

gene: (jeen) *n.* the part of a cell that determines what people look like.

Leticia looks like her parents because she has their **genes**.

generation: (jen-uh-RAY-shun) *n.* a group of individuals who are born during the same time period.

These three women are from different **generations**

genre: (ZHAHN-ruh) *n.* a category of writing or other art forms.

Her favorite literary **genre** is fiction.

gentle: (JENT-ul) *adj.* kind; mild; not rough.

The father was **gentle** when holding his baby.

geography: (jee-AHG-ruh-fee) *n.* the study of the earth and its features, including people, land, and climate.

In **geography** class we learned about the regions of the earth.

geologist: (jee-AHL-uh-jist) *n.* a person who studies the physical history and changes of the earth.

A **geologist** studies rocks to learn more about the earth.

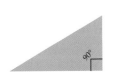

geometry: (jee-AHM-uh-tree) *n.* the branch of mathematics that deals with the properties of points, lines, angles, and other figures.

Using **geometry**, we can calculate the angles of this right triangle.

giraffe: (juh-RAF) *n.* a spotted mammal with an extremely long neck.

The **giraffe** is tall enough to reach leaves at the top of the tree.

girl: (gurl) *n.* a female child.

That **girl** is wearing a pink shirt.

glacier: (GLAY-shur) *n.* a large mass of ice and snow that forms faster than the snow can melt.

This **glacier** is in Alaska.

glad: (glad) *adj.* happy; pleased.

She is **glad** to be on vacation.

glass: (glas) *n.* a container for drinking.

I filled my **glass** with water.

Sounds Like Fun!

Complete this sentence with a "g" word: *The girl gave her grandmother a _____.* Now ask some friends to finish the sentence with other "g" words.

Gg

glasses: (GLAS-iz) *n.* lenses worn to help people see better or more clearly.

She can't see well without her **glasses**.

globe: (glohb) *n.* a round map of the earth.

The class found South America on the **globe**.

glove: (gluv) *n.* a covering for the hand with a section for each finger.

Don't go out in the cold without your **gloves**.

glue: (gloo) *n.* something used to make things stick together.

We used **glue** to make the picture stick to the paper.

goat: (goht) *n.* a horned mammal closely related to sheep.

Goats can climb easily over rocks.

good: (gud) *adj.* better than average.

Peter said the apple tastes **good**.

goose: (goos) *n.* a web-footed bird that swims.

The **goose** can make a very loud honking noise.

gorilla: (guh-RIL-uh) *n.* a large mammal with long arms.

We watched the **gorilla** climb a tree at the zoo.

govern: (GUV-urn) *v.* to rule.

The president of the United States **governs** from the White House.

government: (GUV-urn-munt) *n.* a system of political rule.

The United States **government** is made up of the legislative, judicial, and executive branches.

Gg

graduate: (GRAJ-oo-ayt) *v.* to finish a course of study in a school or college.

Brianna **graduated** from high school in June.

grandfather: (GRAND-fah-<u>thur</u>) *n.* the father of one's parent.

Katie's **grandfather** tells her stories about her dad.

grandmother: (GRAND-mu-<u>thur</u>) *n.* the mother of one's parent.

Alan and April visit their **grandmother** on Thanksgiving.

grape: (grayp) *n.* a small, round fruit that grows in bunches on vines.

We bought a bunch of **grapes** at the store.

grapefruit: (GRAYP-froot) *n.* a large, round citrus fruit.

Nick eats a **grapefruit** for breakfast.

graph: (graf) *n.* a diagram that uses lines or dots to show the relationship between things.

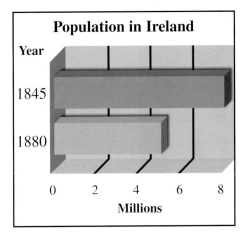

The bar **graph** shows how the population of Ireland decreased in the 1800s.

grass: (gras) *n.* a plant with bladelike leaves.

Rose cuts the **grass** each week.

grasshopper: (GRAS-hahp-ur) *n.* a plant-eating insect with long back legs.

The children found a **grasshopper** in the yard.

79

Gg

grasslands: (GRAS-landz) *n.* an area covered with grass.

This photograph shows some of the **grasslands** in the country of New Zealand.

gravity: (GRAV-uh-tee) *n.* the force that pulls objects toward the center of the earth.

Gravity causes the water to fall to the ground.

great: (grayt) *adj.* extreme in size, number, power, or importance.

Charlemagne was a **great** ruler of the eighth century.

greedy: (GREE-dee) *adj.* wanting more than one's share.

The **greedy** man wanted all the money for himself.

green: (green) *adj.* a color.

This is the color **green**.

guilt: (gilt) *n.* having done something wrong, such as breaking a law.

The police were certain of his **guilt**.

guitar: (gi-TAHR) *n.* a stringed musical instrument.

She plays the **guitar** while her brother sings.

gulf: (guhlf) *n.* a large area of a sea or an ocean that is partly surrounded by land.

Venice, a city in Italy, is located on the **Gulf** of Venice.

gum: (guhm) *n.* a chewy, flavored substance.

We are not allowed to chew **gum** in class.

habitat: (HAB-uh-tat) *n.* the place in nature where a plant or animal lives.

The ocean is the natural **habitat** of whales, dolphins, and sharks.

hair: (hayr) *n.* the thin strands that grow out of the skin, particularly on top of the head.

She has long blonde **hair**.

hairbrush: (HAYR-brush) *n.* something used to arrange hair.

Lisa's hair looked much better after she used the **hairbrush**.

hairdresser: (HAYR-dres-ur) *n.* a person who arranges or cuts hair.

The **hairdresser** curled Lily's hair.

half: (haf) *adj.* one of two equal parts.

We cut the pepper in **half**.

half-dollar: (haf-DAHL-ur) *n.* a U.S. coin worth 50 cents.

Two **half-dollars** equal one dollar.

half-hour: (haf-OWR) *n.* thirty minutes.

The class will last for a **half-hour**.

half-past: (haf-PAST) *adj.* thirty minutes after the hour.

We left school at **half-past** two o'clock.

Hh

ham: (ham) *n.* a meat that comes from pigs.

We ate **ham** at the restaurant.

hamburger: (HAM-bur-gur) *n.* a sandwich containing a ground beef patty.

He bought a **hamburger** for lunch.

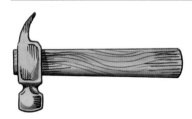

hammer: (HAM-ur) *n.* a tool for hitting nails.

I need a **hammer**, nails, and some wood to fix the hole in the fence.

hand: (hand) *n.* part of the body at the end of the arm containing the wrist and fingers.

Raise your **hand** if you have a question.

happy: (HAP-ee) *adj.* pleased; joyful; glad.

Mrs. Brown was **happy** when she talked to her son

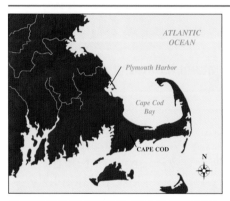

harbor: (HAHR-bur) *n.* a protected part of a body of water that is deep enough for ships.

The first English colonists sailed their ships into Plymouth **Harbor** on the coast of the Atlantic Ocean.

hard: (hahrd) *adj.* not soft; firm and solid.

The rocky ground is **hard**.

harvest: (HAHR-vist) *v.* to gather crops.

The farmer **harvested** the wheat.

hat: (hat) *n.* a covering worn on the head.

She wore this **hat** to the garden party.

head: (hed) *n.* the part of the body containing the skull, brain, mouth, eyes, ears, and nose.

Ramona wore a pink band around her **head**.

healthy: (HEL-thee) *adj.* to be in good health; not sick.

The doctor says she is **healthy**.

eat: (heet) *n.* warmth.

Gladys enjoys the **heat** of a fire on winter nights.

heater: (HEE-tur) *n.* a machine for heating a room.

He uses the **heater** during the winter.

heavy: (HEV-ee) *adj.* of great weight.

He struggled to lift the **heavy** barbell.

heel: (heel) *n.* the back part of the foot.

Her tight shoe made her **heel** hurt.

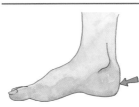

height: (hiyt) *n.* the distance from the bottom to the top of something.

Use a ruler to measure the **height** of the box.

83

helicopter: (HEL-i-kahp-tur) *n.* an aircraft that can lift into the air vertically.

The children were excited to go for a ride in the **helicopter**.

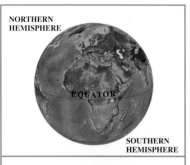

NORTHERN HEMISPHERE
EQUATOR
SOUTHERN HEMISPHERE

WESTERN HEMISPHERE
PRIME MERIDIAN
EASTERN HEMISPHERE

hemisphere: (HEM-uh-sfeer) *n.* half of a sphere divided by a large circle; the earth is divided into the Northern and Southern Hemispheres by the equator and into the Eastern and Western Hemispheres by the prime meridian.

The continent of Africa is located in each of the four **hemispheres**.

hen: (hen) *n.* a bird; a female chicken.

The **hen** laid an egg.

high: (hiy) *adj.* being a great distance from the ground; tall.

The top shelf is too **high** for the boy to reach.

hill: (hil) *n.* a small area of land that is higher than all the land around it; a hill is like a mountain, only much smaller.

We climbed over the **hill**.

hip: (hip) *n.* the part of the body right below the waist.

He placed his hand on his **hip**.

hippopotamus: (hip-uh-PAHT-uh-mus) *n.* a large mammal that has a wide nose and swims in rivers.

The **hippopotamus** walked along the river.

history: (HIS-tuh-ree) *n.* the branch of knowledge dealing with past events.

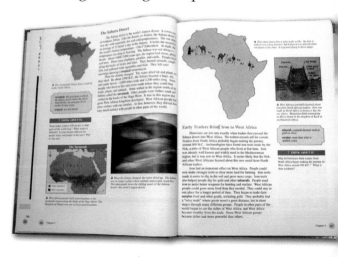

We studied world **history** in class.

hit: (hit) *v.* to strike; to touch with force.

She **hit** the ball with the tennis racquet.

hoe: (hoh) *n.* a long tool used to break up soil.

The gardener used a **hoe** to break up the soil before planting the seeds.

homograph: (HAH-muh-graf) *n.* a word that has the same spelling as another word, but a different meaning and sometimes a different pronunciation.

present (PREZ-unt)   *present* (pri-ZENT)

The noun *present* (gift) and the verb *present* (to bring before an audience) are **homographs**.

homonym: (HAH-muh-nim) *n.* a word that has the same pronunciation and spelling as another word, but a different meaning.

bat (bat)   *bat* (bat)

The word *bat* (animal) and the word *bat* (baseball bat) are **homonyms**.

hoof: (huf) *n.* the hard covering on the foot of an animal.

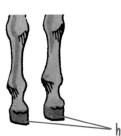

hooves

The horse hurt its **hoof** while it was running.

horizon: (huh-RIY-zun) *n.* the line where the earth and sky seem to meet.

We watched the sun fall below the **horizon**.

horizontal: (hohr-uh-ZAHNT-ul) *adj.* level to the horizon.

He drew a **horizontal** line on the paper.

horse: (hohrs) *n.* a large mammal with hooves and a mane (hair on the neck or shoulders).

The brown and white **horse** walked along the trail.

hose: (hohz) *n.* a tube used to move water to a desired location.

He used the **hose** to water the grass.

Hh

hot: (haht) *adj.* having a high temperature.

She felt **hot** after exercising outdoors in the sun.

hot dog: (haht dawg) *n.* a sandwich containing a type of meat; frankfurter.

I ate a **hot dog** at the baseball game.

hotel: (hoh-TEL) *n.* a place that provides rooms and food for travelers who pay a charge.

They stayed at this **hotel** while on vacation.

hour: (owr) *n.* sixty minutes.

The car trip took one **hour**.

hour hand: (owr hand) *n.* the short hand on a clock or watch.

hour hand

The **hour hand** is on the three.

house: (hows) *n.* a building in which people live.

Our **house** has two bedrooms and a small backyard.

huge: (hyooj) *adj.* very large.

The skyscrapers are **huge**.

human: (HYOO-mun) *n.* a mammal; a person.

Men, women, and children are **human**.

humid: (HYOO-mid) *adj.* moist; wet or damp.

Rain forests are warm and **humid**.

humorous: (HYOO-muhr-us) *adj.* comical; funny.

This picture of a puppy in a mailbox is **humorous**.

hungry: (HUHNG-gree) *adj.* having a desire or need for food.

The dog is **hungry** and wants food in his bowl.

hurricane: (HUR-uh-kayn) *n.* a violent tropical storm.

The **hurricane** blew down houses and flooded the streets.

hyperbole: (hiy-PUR-buh-lee) *n.* an exaggeration.

This box weighs a ton!

Marcus uses **hyperbole** to get people's attention.

hypothesis: (hiy-PAHTH-uh-sis) *n.* something not proven but assumed to be true for the purpose of further study.

I predict....

The scientist will test his **hypothesis** to find out if it's true.

ice: (iys) *n.* frozen water.

Putting **ice** in your drink will keep it cold.

ice cream: (iys kreem) *n.* a frozen dessert made with milk or cream.

On hot days we have **ice cream** for dessert.

ice skate: (iys skayt) *n.* a shoe with a metal blade for skating on ice.

She glided over the ice in these brown **ice skates**.

identification: (iy-den-tuh-fuh-KAY-shun) *n.* a card or piece of paper that shows personal information.

John showed his **identification** so he could buy a student ticket at the movie theater.

idiom: (ID-ee-um) *n.* an expression that doesn't make sense on its own, but has meaning to the people who use it.

The **idiom** "she let the cat out of the bag" means to tell something that should have stayed a secret.

ignore: (ig-NOHR) *v.* to pay no attention to; to disregard.

Adahy **ignores** Lee when she is angry.

ill: (il) *adj.* sick; not well.

Ted stayed home in bed because he felt **ill**.

illustrate: (IL-uh-strayt) *v.* to draw or paint a picture.

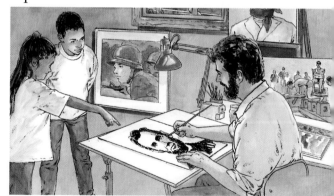

He **illustrated** a picture of President Abraham Lincoln.

imaginary: (i-MAJ-uh-nayr-ee) *adj.* not real.

Boyd's journeys in the sky are **imaginary**.

imitate: (IM-i-tayt) *v.* to follow a model or example; to copy.

Alexis **imitated** the monkey's movements.

immigrant: (IM-i-grunt) *n.* a person who leaves his or her country to live in another country.

Many Irish **immigrants** came to the United States in the 1800s.

immunization: (im-yuh-ni-ZAY-shun) *n.* treatment to help keep a person from getting an illness.

The nurse is giving **immunizations** for the measles.

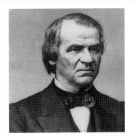

impeach: (im-PEECH) *v.* to make a formal charge that a public official has done something wrong.

Congress **impeached** President Andrew Johnson for breaking a law.

imperialism: (im-PEER-ee-uh-liz-um) *n.* when one country conquers and rules another country.

Leaders of the Roman empire were interested in conquering new lands as part of their policy of **imperialism**.

impolite: (im-puh-LIYT) *adj.* not polite; rude.

It is **impolite** to take someone else's food.

import: (im-POHRT) *v.* to bring goods from another country or place.

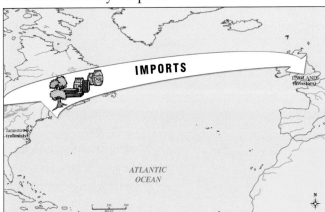

England **imported** lumber and farm supplies from the American colonies.

89

important: (im-POHR-tunt) *adj.* significant.

The president of the United States makes many **important** speeches.

in: (in) *prep.* within a space.

She put the eggs **in** the basket.

inch: (inch) *n.* a unit of length equal to $\frac{1}{12}$ of a foot.

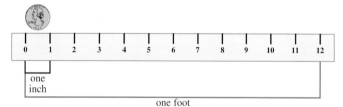

one inch

one foot

One **inch** is about the width of a quarter.

income: (in-KUM) *n.* money that a person receives for doing work or providing services.

Megan gives most of her **income** to her parents to help pay for college.

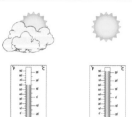

increase: (in-KREES) *v.* to make or become greater.

The temperature **increased** in the afternoon as the sun got brighter.

independent: (in-di-PEN-dunt) *adj.* not under the rule or control of another.

The people in the American colonies wanted to become **independent** of Great Britain.

indicate: (IN-di-kayt) *v.* to point out or show.

This sign **indicates** where it is safe to cross the street.

industry: (IN-duh-stree) *n.* companies that make things.

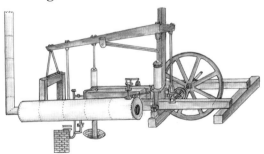

The invention of the steam engine had an important effect on **industry** in the United States.

inflation: (in-FLAY-shun) *n.* a rise in the price of goods and services.

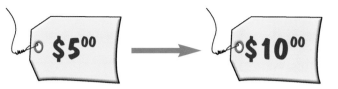

Inflation makes it harder for people to buy the things they need.

ingredient: (in-GREE-dee-unt) *n.* an item that goes into a mixture.

Lemons are the main **ingredient** in lemonade.

injure: (IN-jur) *v.* to harm or hurt.

Randy **injured** his arm on the playground.

insect: (IN-sekt) *n.* a small, often winged animal such as a fly, ladybug, ant, and grasshopper.

This picture shows four different types of **insects**.

inside: (in-SIYD) *prep.* on the inner part; within.

The dog sleeps **inside** the doghouse.

inspect: (in-SPEKT) *v.* to look at carefully; to examine.

He **inspects** frogs and bugs to learn more about them.

install: (in-STAWL) *v.* to set up or connect for use.

The workers **installed** a new roof on our house.

institution: (in-stuh-TOO-shun) *n.* an established organization.

The university is an **institution** of learning.

Ii

Internet: (IN-tur-net) *n.* the connection of computers all over the world through which information can be shared.

He searched the **Internet** for information about Mexican culture.

interrupt: (in-tuh-RUHPT) *v.* to break into the middle of something.

The news report **interrupted** the television program.

intersect: (in-tur-SEKT) *v.* to cut across or through.

These lines **intersect** at a point.

into: (IN-too) *prep.* to the inside of.

He put money **into** the vending machine.

introduce: (in-truh-DOOS) *v.* to identify and present two people to each other.

She **introduced** her friend to her father.

invent: (in-VENT) *v.* to create for the first time.

Eli Whitney **invented** the cotton gin to separate the cotton fibers from the seeds.

invention: (in-VEN-shun) *n.* a new device or process.

The **invention** of the airplane made human flight possible.

investigate: (in-VES-ti-gayt) *v.* to study in close detail.

The detective **investigated** the crime.

Sounds Like Fun!

How many of the words on this page have four syllables? Three syllables? Two syllables?

invisible: (in-VIZ-uh-bul) *adj.* impossible to see.

The movie was about an **invisible** man.

iron: (IY-urn) *n.* an appliance that is heated and used to press clothes smooth.

I used the **iron** to remove the wrinkles from my shirt and pants.

ironing board: (IY-ur-ning bohrd) *n.* a flat board on which clothes or other materials are ironed to remove any wrinkles.

I spread the shirt out smoothly on the **ironing board** before I ironed it.

irrigation: (ir-uh-GAY-shun) *n.* the process of supplying land with water.

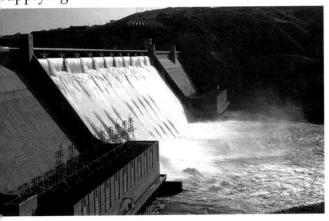

Dams, such as the one in this picture, can be used for **irrigation**.

irritate: (IR-uh-tayt) *v.* to make sensitive or sore.

Poison oak **irritates** my skin and causes it to itch.

island: (IY-lund) *n.* land surrounded by water on all sides.

Japan is made up of four main **islands**.

isolate: (IY-suh-layt) *v.* to set or keep apart.

The sick mouse was **isolated** from the other mice.

Jj

jacket: (JAK-it) *n.* a short coat.

I wear my blue **jacket** during the winter.

jam: (jam) *n.* a thick spread of crushed fruit.

I like **jam** on my toast.

January: (JAN-yoo-er-ee) *n.* the first month of the year.

A new year begins each **January**.

jaw: (jaw) *n.* the part of the body that forms the frame of the mouth.

We move our **jaw** when we eat.

jeep: (jeep) *n.* a vehicle that can drive on uneven roads.

The soldier drove the **jeep** through the jungle.

jello: (JEL-oh) *n.* a dessert made from gelatin and fruit flavoring.

The cafeteria serves lime **jello** on Tuesdays.

jelly: (JEL-ee) *n.* a thin spread made from fruit juice.

I just bought a new jar of strawberry **jelly**.

jet: (jet) *n.* an airplane with a jet engine.

We flew to California in a **jet**.

journey: (JUR-nee) *n.* a trip from one place to another.

Leo Africanus wrote about his **journeys** in Africa.

Dictionary Detective

The word *jam* has more than one meaning. Look up *jam* in a standard dictionary and find out the other meanings of this word. Choose one of these meanings and use it in a sentence.

joy: (joi) *adj.* a feeling of great happiness.

Mona felt **joy** when she held her baby granddaughter.

judge: (juhj) *n.* a public officer who hears and decides court cases.

The **judge** told the jury to listen carefully.

uice: (joos) *n.* a liquid that comes from fruit.

We drank orange **juice** this morning.

July: (ju-LIY) *n.* the seventh month of the year.

Americans celebrate Independence Day on **July** 4th.

jump rope: (juhmp rohp) *n.* a rope used for exercise or fun.

He jumped over the **jump rope** 100 times without falling.

June: (joon) *n.* the sixth month of the year.

Many people graduate from school in **June**.

jury: (JOOR-ee) *n.* a group of people who agree to look for the truth and make a decision about some matter.

The **jury** listened to all the evidence in the court case.

justice: (JUHS-tis) *n.* fairness.

People expect **justice** when they go to a court of law.

95

Kk

kangaroo: (kang-guh-ROO) *n.* a mammal with powerful back legs and a long, thick tail.

We saw a **kangaroo** on our trip to Australia.

key: (kee) *n.* a small metal object designed to fit into a lock.

We cannot get inside the house without the **key**.

keyboard: (KEE-bohrd) *n.* a set of buttons arranged in rows for operating a computer.

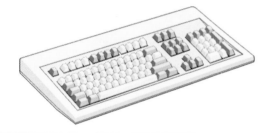

She could not type her report because the **keyboard** was broken.

kind: (kiynd) *adj.* wanting to do good; considerate.

The **kind** boy helped the injured dog.

king: (king) *n.* a male leader or ruler.

The **king** wears a crown at important ceremonies.

kitchen: (KICH-un) *n.* a room where food is cooked.

We cooked dinner in the **kitchen**.

kite: (kiyt) *n.* a lightweight frame covered with thin material that is flown in the wind on the end of a long string.

We flew the blue **kite** in the park.

kitten: (KIT-un) *n.* a mammal; a young cat.

The **kitten** likes to sit on my lap.

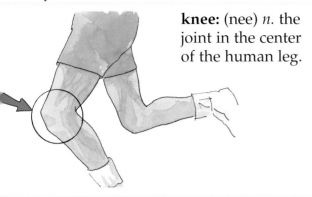

knee: (nee) *n.* the joint in the center of the human leg.

His **knee** is sore from running.

knife: (niyf) *n.* a tool with a blade for cutting.

He cut the sandwich with a **knife**.

knock: (nahk) *v.* to make a pounding noise.

William **knocked** on the door.

ladder: (LAD-ur) *n.* a wooden or metal structure used to reach high places.

She used a **ladder** to reach the ceiling.

ladybug: (LAY-dee-buhg) *n.* a small, spotted insect.

The **ladybug** crawled across the leaf.

lake: (layk) *n.* a large body of water completely surrounded by land.

We went fishing in the **lake**.

lamb: (lam) *n.* a mammal; a young sheep.

The **lamb** lives on a farm.

lamp: (lamp) *n.* a device that produces light.

She turned on the **lamp** when the room became dark.

bird

ibon

鳥   con chim   pájaro

noog   *oiseau*

language: (LANG-gwij) *n.* the system of words used by a group of people.

I can write the word *bird* in seven **languages**.

large: (lahrj) *adj.* big.

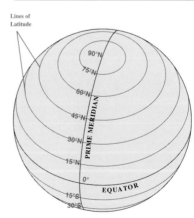

These are the bones from a **large** dinosaur.

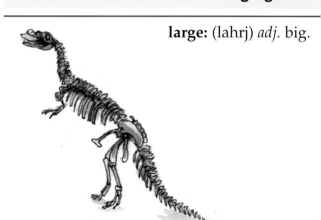

latitude: (LAT-uh-tood) *n.* the imaginary lines north and south of the equator that are used to measure distance; lines of latitude are sometimes called "parallels."

Most maps show only a few lines of **latitude**, but geographers have divided the earth into 180 lines of **latitude**.

98

laugh: (laf) *v.* a reaction expressed when someone thinks something is funny.

The joke made Cynthia **laugh** out loud.

law: (law) *n.* a rule that people must follow.

The courts decide whether a **law** has been broken.

ay: (lay) *v.* to set down.

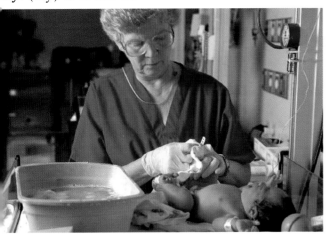

The nurse **lays** all new babies on this table.

lazy: (LAY-zee) *adj.* not willing to work.

Sam took the day off because he felt **lazy**.

left: (left) *adj.* on the same side of the body as the heart.

Left

Julio looked to the **left**.

leg: (leg) *n.* one of the two lower limbs on a human being.

He stretches each **leg** before running.

legend: (LEJ-und) *n.* an old story that is widely believed but cannot be proven.

The **legend** of Johnny Appleseed tells about one man's journeys in the American West.

legislature: (LEJ-is-lay-chur) *n.* a group of elected people who have the power to make or change laws.

The U.S. **legislature** meets in the Capitol in Washington, D.C.

lemon: (LEM-un) *n.* a yellow citrus fruit that has a sour taste.

We picked **lemons** from the tree and used them to make lemonade.

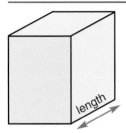

length: (lengkth) *n.* the distance from one end to the other of the long side of an object.

Use a ruler to measure the **length** of this box.

leopard: (LEP-urd) *n.* a large, spotted mammal; a wild cat.

The **leopard** rested on the tree branch.

less: (les) *adj.* a smaller amount.

The mom has **less** fruit to hold than her daughter.

letter: (LET-ur) *n.* a written communication.

Sandra wrote a **letter** to her friend.

lettuce: (LET-us) *n.* a leafy plant used for salads.

We put **lettuce** and tomatoes in the salad.

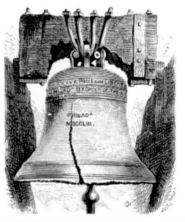

liberty: (LIB-ur-tee) *n.* freedom and independence.

The famous Liberty Bell in Philadelphia is a symbol of **liberty** in the United States.

librarian: (liy-BRAYR-ee-un) *n.* a person who helps people find books and other information in a library.

The **librarian** helped me find books about space travel.

library: (LIY-brayr-ee) *n.* a place containing books, recordings, and other materials.

She went to the **library** to find a book about famous inventors.

lie: (liy) *v.* to rest flat.

The cat likes to **lie** on the floor.

lifeguard: (LIYF-gahrd) *n.* a person whose job it is to protect swimmers from drowning and other accidents.

The **lifeguard** works at the beach all summer.

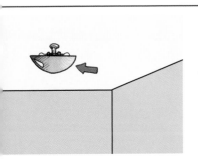

light: (liyt) *n.* a device that makes a room bright.

He turned on the **light** when he entered the room.

line: (liyn) *n.* a long, thin mark.

She began her picture by drawing a green **line**.

lion: (LIY-un) *n.* a large light brown mammal; a wild cat.

Male **lions** have a lot of hair on their necks and shoulders.

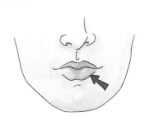

lip: (lip) *n.* the part of the body that forms the upper or lower edges of the mouth.

The cold air made her **lips** dry.

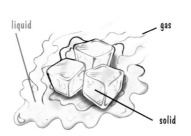

liquid   gas

solid

liquid: (LIK-wid) *n.* anything that can flow like water; not a solid or gas.

When the ice melted, it became a **liquid**.

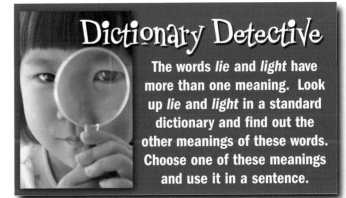

Dictionary Detective

The words *lie* and *light* have more than one meaning. Look up *lie* and *light* in a standard dictionary and find out the other meanings of these words. Choose one of these meanings and use it in a sentence.

literature: (LIT-ur-uh-chur) *n.* written works such as novels and poems.

We are reading early American **literature** in class.

little: (LIT-ul) *adj.* small.

The insect is **little** compared to the girl.

living room: (LIV-ing room) *n.* a room in a house where people sit and talk.

We sit in the **living room** when friends visit our house.

lizard: (LIZ-urd) *n.* a scaly reptile with a long tail.

Lizards live in places that have warm climates.

locate: (LOH-kayt) *v.* to look for and find an exact place or thing.

The teacher helped the students **locate** South America on the world map.

lock: (lahk) *n.* a device for securing a door, drawer, or other item.

I use this **lock** when I park my bike at school.

logic: (LAHJ-ik) *n.* thinking in a reasonable way.

People use **logic** to solve math problems.

lonely: (LOHN-lee) *adj.* a sad feeling of being alone.

He felt **lonely** on the island by himself.

long: (lahng) *adj.* of great length.

The giraffe's **long** neck helps it reach high branches.

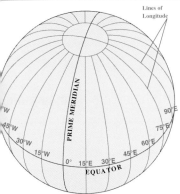

longitude: (LAHN-juh-tood) *n.* the imaginary lines east and west of the prime meridian that are used to measure distance; lines of longitude are sometimes called "meridians."

Most maps show only a few lines of **longitude**, but geographers have divided the earth into 360 lines of **longitude**.

look: (luk) *v.* to turn one's eyes toward something in order to see it.

She **looked** inside the chest.

loud: (lowd) *adj.* noisy; not quiet in sound.

The trumpet makes a **loud** sound.

low: (loh) *adj.* placed close to the ground; not high.

The **low** shelf is easier to reach than the high shelf.

lunch: (luhnch) *n.* a light meal in the middle of the day.

She ate a sandwich and potato chips for **lunch**.

Mm

machine: (muh-SHEEN) *n.* a piece of equipment that is used to do a job.

The cotton spinning **machine** helped make clothes faster.

magazine: (MAG-uh-zeen) *n.* a paperbound publication containing stories, pictures, and other news.

Mark likes to read the sports articles in *Kids Today* **magazine**.

magnify: (MAG-ni-fiy) *v.* to make something appear bigger.

Inga used a magnifying glass to **magnify** the small insect.

mail carrier: (mayl KAYR-ee-ur) *n.* a person whose job is to deliver letters and other mail.

The **mail carrier** brought us two letters and a postcard.

mail truck: (mayl truhk) *n.* a vehicle used to deliver letters and other mail.

The **mail truck** is filled with mail for the people in the city.

104

make: (mayk) *v.* to form out of material or parts.

Tess **makes** cards for Valentine's Day.

mammal: (MAM-ul) *n.* a warm-blooded animal that has hair and feeds its young with milk.

Humans, lions, dogs, and whales are all **mammals**.

man: (man) *n.* an adult male.

This **man** is Diego's father.

manufacture: (MAN-yuh-fak-chur) *v.* to make products by hand or machine.

This is where cars are **manufactured**.

many: (MEN-ee) *adj.* a large number.

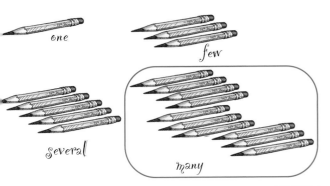

The teacher brought **many** pencils for the students in her class.

map: (map) *n.* an illustration of all or part of the earth.

This is a **map** of the United States.

March: (mahrch) *n.* the third month of the year.

In **March**, the weather in some parts of the United States begins to get warmer.

match: (mach) *v.* to identify two things that are exactly like or equal.

two	2

The object of this game is to **match** the number word with the numeral.

mathematics: (MATH-uh-mat-iks) *n.* the science that deals with numbers; also called "math."

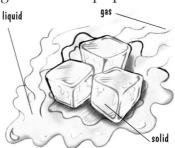

We learned how to add fractions in our **mathematics** class.

matter: (MAT-ur) *n.* what things are made of; something that takes up space and has weight.

Gas, liquids, and solids are the three forms of **matter**.

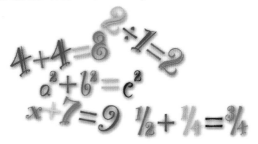

May: (may) *n.* the fifth month of the year.

We celebrate Mother's Day in **May**.

Dictionary Detective

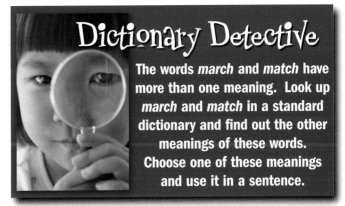

The words *march* and *match* have more than one meaning. Look up *march* and *match* in a standard dictionary and find out the other meanings of these words. Choose one of these meanings and use it in a sentence.

Mm

mean: (meen) 1. *n.* an average. 2. *adj.* purposely unkind; not nice.

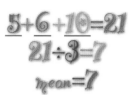

| 1. In this example, the **mean** is seven. | 2. It was **mean** of Liz to trip Henry. |

---

measure: (MEZH-ur) *v.* to find out the size or amount of something.

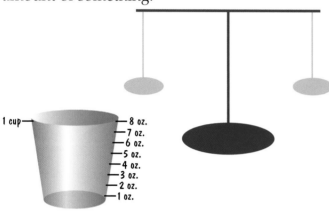

We use scales, measuring cups, and rulers to **measure** different things.

---

meat: (meet) *n.* the flesh of an animal used for food.

Steak and sausage are types of **meat**.

mechanic: (mi-KAN-ik) *n.* a person whose job is to repair machines.

The **mechanic** fixed the broken car.

media: (MEE-dee-uh) *n.* the tools through which something is communicated.

Televisions, magazines, newspapers, and radios are all forms of **media**.

---

median: (MEE-dee-un) *n.* the middle number in a series of numbers.

3, 5, 6, 8, 10

In the example, the **median** is 6.

---

medieval: (MED-ee-vul) *adj.* relating to the Middle Ages, the period of European history from about A.D. 500 to 1500.

In **medieval** times, knights promised loyalty to their king.

medium-sized: (MEE-dee-um-siyzd) *adj.* being in the middle in terms of amount; in between big and small.

He ordered a **medium-sized** drink.

mesa: (MAY-suh) *n.* a small, flat-topped area of land that is higher than the land around it and has one or more clifflike sides.

The American Indians of the Southwest region of North America built their homes on **mesas**.

metaphor: (MET-uh-fohr) *n.* a figure of speech that compares two unlike things without using the words *like* or *as*.

Using **metaphors** such as "Your lips are rubies" can make your writing more interesting.

metric system: (MET-rik SIS-tum) *n.* a system of weights and measures.

Centimeters are units of measurement in the **metric system**.

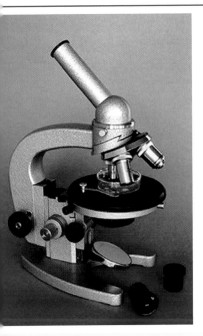

microscope: (MIY-kruh-skohp) *n.* an instrument that makes very small objects appear larger.

The scientist uses the **microscope** to study bacteria.

microwave oven: (MIY-kruh-wayv UHV-un) *n.* an oven that uses electrical waves to heat food.

We can make popcorn quickly in a **microwave oven**.

middle: (MID-ul) *n.* in the center.

Cecily is standing in the **middle**.

migrant: (MIY-grunt) *adj.* moving from region to region.

The **migrant** workers will move to northern California when it is time to harvest grapes.

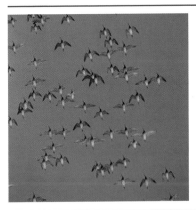

migrate: (MIY-grayt) v. to move from region to region on a regular schedule.

Every year these birds **migrate** south for the winter.

Mm

mile: (miyl) *n.* a measure of distance equal to 5,280 feet, or a little over 1½ kilometers.

The speed limit tells you to go no faster than 45 **miles** per hour.

milk: (milk) *n.* a white liquid used for food that comes from cows, goats, or other female mammals.

I like to drink **milk** when I eat cookies.

mineral: (MIN-ur-ul) *n.* a solid substance that is found in rocks.

Gold is a type of **mineral**.

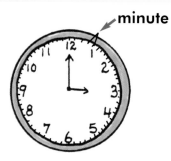

minute: (MIN-it) *n.* 60 seconds.

The commercial on television lasted one **minute**.

minute hand: (MIN-it hand) *n.* the long hand on a clock or watch.

The **minute hand** is on the 12.

mirror: (MEER-ur) *n.* a reflecting surface, usually made of glass.

Celia looked at herself in the **mirror**.

mitten: (MIT-un) *n.* a hand covering with one section for the thumb and another section for all four fingers.

Lucy wears her red **mittens** when she plays in the snow.

My Very Excellent
Mother Just Served
Us Nutritious Pears.

Mercury, Venus,
Earth, Mars, Jupiter,
Saturn, Uranus,
Neptune, Pluto

mnemonic: (ni-MAHN-ik) *n.* something used to help the memory.

The **mnemonic**, "My Very Excellent Mother Just Served Us Nutritious Pears," helps us remember the names and order of the planets in our solar system.

moccasin: (MAHK-uh-sin) *n.* a shoe made of soft leather originally worn by American Indians.

The **moccasins** were soft and comfortable.

1, 2, 2, 3, 2, 1
mode = 2

mode: (mohd) *n.* the number that appears most frequently in a set of numbers.

In this example, the **mode** is two.

modern: (MAHD-urn) *adj.* relating to or characteristic of present times or times not long past.

This sculpture is an example of **modern** art.

oxygen atom

hydrogen atoms

molecule: (MAHL-uh-kyool) *n.* the smallest part of a substance that has the properties of that substance.

A water **molecule** is made up of two hydrogen atoms and one oxygen atom.

monarchy: (MAHN-uhr-kee) *n.* a system of government in which a king or queen rules.

King or Queen

People

France had a **monarchy** under King Louis XIV.

Monday: (MUHN-day) *n.* the day of the week after Sunday and before Tuesday.

On **Monday**, we start a new week at school.

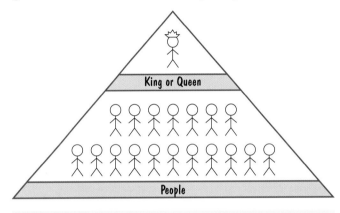

money: (MUHN-ee) *n.* printed paper or stamped metal used for buying and selling goods.

He used the **money** to buy food.

109

Mm

monitor: (MAHN-uh-tur) *n.* a computer part with a screen.

As you type the words on the keyboard, you will see them appear on the **monitor**.

monkey: (MUHN-kee) *n.* a mammal with fur, a flat face, and usually a long tail.

The **monkey** was sitting in a tree.

moon: (moon) *n.* the object that revolves around the earth and reflects light from the sun.

If the sky is clear tonight, we will see a full **moon**.

moose: (moos) *n.* a large mammal; a type of deer with antlers and humped shoulders.

We saw a **moose** in the woods.

mop: (mahp) *n.* an object with a long handle and sponge or bundle of yarn used for cleaning floors.

You can use the **mop** to clean up the juice that spilled on the floor.

more: (mohr) *adj.* a greater amount or number.

Danae has **more** oranges than her mother.

mosquito: (muh-SKEE-toh) *n.* an insect—the female sucks the blood of people and animals.

I was bitten by a **mosquito** on our camping trip.

mother: (MUHTH-ur) *n.* a female parent.

Julie's **mother** walks her to school each day.

Dictionary Detective

Monitor can also be used as a verb. Look up *monitor* in a standard dictionary to find out the verb form of the word. Then use *monitor* as a verb in a sentence.

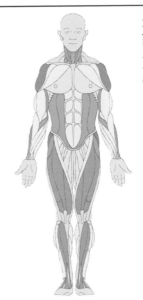

motorcycle: (MOH-tur-siy-kul) *n.* a motor vehicle with two wheels.

Ted always wears a helmet when he rides his **motorcycle**.

mountain: (MOWN-tun) *n.* a very high, natural elevation of the earth's surface, with steep sides.

Early European settlers in America crossed **mountains** as they moved westward.

mouse: (mows) *n.* 1. a small mammal with a long, thin tail. 2. a small device used to select items on a computer screen.

1. The **mouse** ran into the hole.

2. Click the **mouse** to select the computer program you want to use.

mouth: (mowth) *n.* the part of the body that allows a person to talk, eat, and breathe.

Angela put the ice cream in her **mouth**.

moving van: (MOO-ving van) *n.* a vehicle used to move furniture and other household items from one place to another.

Ben loaded all his furniture into the **moving van**.

multiplication: (mul-tuh-pli-KAY-shun) *n.* the process of adding a number to itself several times.

Using **multiplication**, we know that five times six equals 30.

muscle: (MUHS-ul) *n.* body tissue that makes it possible for a person or animal to move.

Muscles make it possible for your arms to bend and your fingers to move.

Mm

museum: (myoo-ZEE-um) *n.* a building in which items of scientific interest or objects of art are displayed.

The students went on a field trip to the **museum**.

musician: (myoo-ZISH-un) *n.* a person who plays a musical instrument.

The **musician** played a beautiful song on the violin.

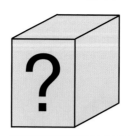

mystery: (MIS-tuh-ree) *n.* something that is unexplained or secret.

The contents of this box are a **mystery**.

myth: (mith) *n.* a legend about someone who has great powers; myths sometimes explain a custom or religious belief.

In Roman **myths**, Venus is the goddess of love.

nail: (nayl) *n.* a slender piece of metal made to be hammered into wood or other material.

We used a hammer and **nail** to hang the picture on the wall.

napkin: (NAP-kin) *n.* a piece of cloth or paper used to clean the lips and hands while eating.

Maya used a **napkin** to protect her clothes while she ate.

narrator: (NAYR-ay-tur) *n.* a person who tells a story.

The **narrator** told the story as his classmates acted out the scene.

narrow: (NAYR-oh) *adj.* of little width; a slender space.

The space between these green lines is **narrow**.

near: (neer) *adj.* close in distance or time.

The penguins stood **near** each other.

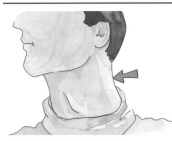

neck: (nek) *n.* the part of the body that connects the head to the rest of the body.

Patrick had a sore **neck** when he woke up in the morning.

necklace: (NEK-lis) *n.* a piece of jewelry worn around the neck.

Sandra wears this **necklace** on special occasions.

neglect: (ni-GLEKT) *v.* to fail to give enough attention or care to someone or something.

The owners **neglected** this barn for many years.

Nn

neighborhood: (NAY-bur-hud) *n.* a place in which people live near one another.

Many families in our **neighborhood** decorate their houses for the holidays.

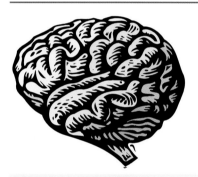

nerve: (nurv) *n.* something that connects to the brain and carries messages throughout the body.

Nerves in the brain allow us to feel such things as hot and cold, pain, and motion.

new: (noo) *adj.* not old; recent.

Yuko bought a **new** pink dress to wear to the party.

news carrier: (nooz KAYR-ee-ur) *n.* a person whose job is to deliver newspapers.

The **news carrier** put the newspaper in front of our door.

newspaper: (NOOZ-pay-pur) *n.* a daily or weekly publication containing news, sports, and advertising.

I read an interesting story in today's **newspaper**.

next to: (nekst too) *prep.* beside; near.

She stood **next to** the table.

nice: (niys) *adj.* pleasant; kind.

It was **nice** of Malcolm to share his lunch.

nickel: (NIK-ul) *n.* a U.S. coin worth five cents.

Sam is saving his **nickels** to buy candy.

114

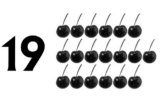

nine: (niyn) *n.* a number equaling eight plus one; numbers are usually used as adjectives in a sentence.

The family bought **nine** bananas.

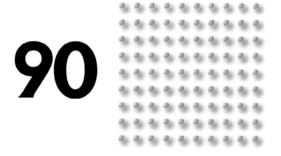

nineteen: (niyn-TEEN) *n.* a number equaling 10 plus nine; numbers are usually used as adjectives in a sentence.

She ate **nineteen** cherries.

ninety: (NIYN-tee) *n.* a number equaling 10 times nine; numbers are usually used as adjectives in a sentence.

90

Ten rows of nine dots make a total of **ninety** dots.

ninth: (niynth) *adj.* that which follows the eighth.

The **ninth** owl landed on the tree branch.

noisy: (NOI-zee) *adj.* loud.

Pots and pans make **noisy** toys.

nomadic: (noh-MAD-ik) *adj.* relating to people who do not have a permanent home, but instead move from place to place.

Nomadic groups have lived in the deserts of Arabia for thousands of years.

nonfiction: (nahn-FIK-shun) *n.* writings that contain facts and are true.

This history book is an example of **nonfiction**.

north: (nohrth) *n.* the direction opposite of south.

On most maps, **north** is towards the top.

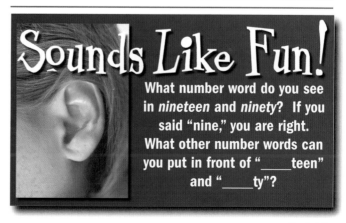

Sounds Like Fun!

What number word do you see in *nineteen* and *ninety*? If you said "nine," you are right. What other number words can you put in front of "_____teen" and "_____ty"?

Nn

nose: (nohz) *n.* the part of the body that allows a person to breathe and smell.

When Barbara was sick, she couldn't breathe through her **nose**.

novel: (NAHV-ul) *n.* a book that tells a made-up story.

The **novel** *Little Women* tells the story of four sisters.

November: (noh-VEM-bur) *n.* the eleventh month of the year.

Americans celebrate Thanksgiving in **November**.

nucleus: (NOO-klee-us) *n.* the part of a cell that contains chromosomes.

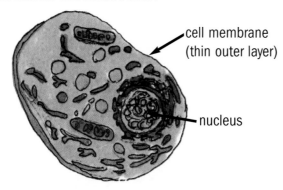

cell membrane (thin outer layer)

nucleus

The scientist studied the **nucleus** of a plant cell to find out more about it.

number: (NUHM-bur) *n.* a symbol that represents an amount.

We work with **numbers** in mathematics.

nurse: (nurs) *n.* a person trained to care for hurt or sick people.

The **nurse** put a bandage on Samantha's arm.

nut: (nuht) *n.* a food that has a kernel inside a shell.

Roberta cannot eat **nuts** because they make her very sick.

nutrient: (NOO-tree-unt) *n.* a substance that helps animals and plants live and grow.

Milk contains calcium, an important **nutrient** for strong bones.

object: (AWB-jikt) *n.* something that may be seen or felt.

He had to remove the paper and other **objects** from his desk.

obstacle: (AWB-stuh-kul) *n.* something that stands in the way; a barrier.

The dog did not let the **obstacle** get in his way.

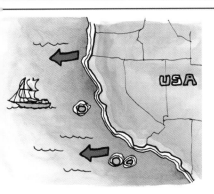

occasionally: (uh-KAY-shuhn-uhl-ee) *adv.* from time to time; now and then.

We **occasionally** go to the movies.

ocean: (OH-shun) *n.* a vast body of salt water.

Boats sail on the **ocean**.

October: (ahk-TOH-bur) *n.* the tenth month of the year.

Halloween is always on **October** 31.

octopus: (AHK-tuh-pus) *n.* an invertebrate (an animal without a backbone) that lives in the ocean and has a soft body and eight arms.

We saw an **octopus** at the aquarium.

off: (awf) *prep.* away from the surface or top of.

The phone is **off** the hook.

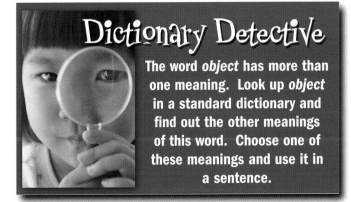

Dictionary Detective

The word *object* has more than one meaning. Look up *object* in a standard dictionary and find out the other meanings of this word. Choose one of these meanings and use it in a sentence.

Oo

office: (AW-fis) *n.* an area where business takes place.

The teacher asked him to take a note to the principal's **office**.

old: (ohld) *adj.* having lived or existed for a long time.

Some **old** Roman buildings, such as the Colosseum, still stand today.

on: (awn) *prep.* in contact with.

The cat sat **on** the bench.

on top of: (awn tahp uhv) *prep.* over and in contact with.

The bird is **on top of** the lion's head.

one: (wuhn) *n.* a number indicating a single unit; numbers are usually used as adjectives in a sentence.

We need **one** soccer ball and two goals to play soccer.

one hundred: (wuhn HUN-drid) *n.* a number equaling 10 times 10; numbers are usually used as adjectives in a sentence.

100

Ten rows of 10 dots make a total of **one hundred** dots.

onion: (UHN-yun) *n.* a vegetable with a strong smell and taste.

Pedro used **onions**, peppers, and steak to make fajitas for dinner.

opinion: (uh-PIN-yun) *n.* a personal belief or view.

That was a great movie.

Talia's **opinion** is that the movie was great.

orange: (OHR-inj) 1. *adj.* a color. 2. *n.* a sweet citrus fruit.

1. This is the color **orange**.

2. She picked an **orange** from the tree.

orbit: (OHR-bit) *v.* to move in a circle around a planet, the sun, or another heavenly body.

The satellite **orbits** the earth.

orchestra: (OHR-ki-struh) *n.* a group of musicians playing instruments.

The **orchestra** played a song written by Beethoven.

organ: (OHR-gun) *n.* a part of the body that has a certain function or job.

The brain is the **organ** that allows us to think.

organism: (OHR-guh-niz-um) *n.* a living being, including people, animals, and plants.

Plants and animals are two types of **organisms**.

organize: (OHR-guh-niyz) *v.* to arrange in an orderly way.

Mrs. Wilks **organized** the student records in a file cabinet.

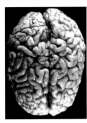

ostrich: (AHS-trich) *n.* a tall bird that cannot fly but is able to run quickly.

The **ostrich** has a long neck and long legs.

Dictionary Detective

The word *organ* has more than one meaning. Look up *organ* in a standard dictionary and find out the other meanings of this word. Choose one of these meanings and use it in a sentence.

119

Oo

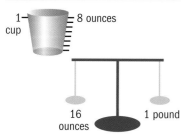

ounce: (owns) *n.* a unit of measurement or weight equal to ⅛ cup or 1/16 pound.

The cook put four **ounces** of butter in the cake mix.

out: (owt) *prep.* located away from the inside.

Marissa took the turtle **out** of the cage.

outside: (owt-SIYD) *prep.* outdoors; a place beyond an enclosed area.

The children like to play **outside** after school.

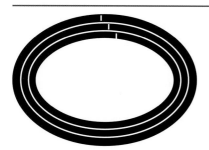

oval: (OH-vul) *n.* an egg shape.

The running track is in the shape of an **oval**.

over: (OH-vur) *prep.* above; higher than.

The picture is **over** the couch.

owl: (owl) *n.* a bird with a large head and strong claws.

The brown **owl** is sitting on the branch.

oxygen: (AHK-si-jun) *n.* a colorless, odorless gas found in the air that is needed for life.

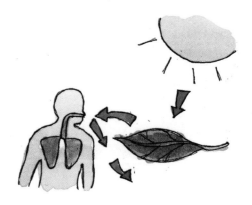

Humans breathe in **oxygen** and breathe out carbon dioxide; plants take in carbon dioxide and release oxygen.

package: (PAK-ij) *n.* a bundle that is boxed or wrapped.

Francis' parents sent her this **package** for her birthday.

page: (payj) *n.* one side of a sheet of paper in a book, magazine, or other printed item.

There are 256 **pages** in our history textbook.

pail: (payl) *n.* a round container with a handle; a bucket.

She filled the blue **pail** with water.

painter: (PAYN-tur) *n.* a person whose job is to paint.

The **painter** is almost finished painting the room white.

pair: (payr) *n.* two things that are matched and used together.

I bought this **pair** of shoes for running.

pajamas: (puh-JAH-muhz) *n.* loose-fitting clothes worn for sleeping.

Dion changed into his blue **pajamas** before going to bed.

pan: (pan) *n.* a container with a handle used in cooking.

Andrew heated the sauce in a **pan**.

pancake: (PAN-kayk) *n.* a thin, flat cake, often served with butter and syrup.

Victoria ate **pancakes** for breakfast.

pants: (pants) *n.* clothing worn on the legs; trousers.

Jim bought new **pants** to wear to work.

paper: (PAY-pur) *n.* sheets used for writing or drawing.

I wrote my book report on lined **paper**.

paragraph: (PAYR-uh-graf) *n.* a group of sentences about one topic.

This page has two **paragraphs**.

parallel: (PAYR-uh-lel) *adj.* moving in the same direction and always remaining the same distance apart.

These lines are **parallel**.

parasite: (PAYR-uh-siyt) *n.* a plant or animal that lives on or in another living thing and gets food from it.

Fleas are **parasites** sometimes found on cats and dogs.

parrot: (PAYR-ut) *n.* a bird with colorful feathers.

Lindy taught her pet **parrot** to say "hello."

passenger: (PAS-un-jur) *n.* a person who travels in or on a vehicle.

This man is a **passenger** on the train.

past: (past) *n.* a time that has gone by.

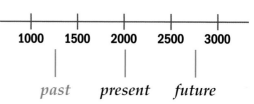

In history class, we study the **past**.

paste: (payst) *n.* a sticky substance used to make paper or other materials stick together.

The students used **paste** in their art class.

patience: (PAY-shuns) *n.* the ability to wait for something without getting angry.

Fishing requires a lot of **patience**.

patio: (PAT-ee-oh) *n.* a paved area outside a house used for outdoor dining or relaxing.

During the summer, we eat on the **patio**.

patriotism: (PAY-tree-uh-tiz-um) *n.* love of one's country.

One way Americans show their **patriotism** is by saying the pledge of allegiance to the American flag.

pea: (pee) *n.* a round, green vegetable.

Peas contain important nutrients.

peacefully: (PEES-fuhl-lee) *adv.* acting in a way that brings about calmness, not conflict.

For many years, the Indians and the pilgrims lived together **peacefully**.

peacock: (PEE-kahk) *n.* a male bird with long, colorful tail feathers.

This **peacock** has beautiful blue tail feathers.

123

Pp

peanut butter: (PEE-nut BUHT-ur) *n.* a spread made from ground peanuts.

Maria eats **peanut butter** sandwiches for lunch.

pear: (payr) *n.* a fruit that is narrow on top and wide on the bottom.

This **pear** is soft.

peasant: (PEZ-unt) *n.* a worker on a farm or person who owns and works on a small farm.

The **peasants** worked hard to grow enough food to feed themselves.

pencil: (PEN-sul) *n.* an object used for writing.

You will need a **pencil** for the test.

pencil sharpener: (PEN sul SHAHRP-uhn-ur) *n.* an object used to make the point on a pencil sharp.

The **pencil sharpener** is in Mrs. O'Brien's classroom

penguin: (PEN-gwin *n.* a black and white bird that does not fly

Penguins can swim under water.

peninsula: (puh-NIN-suh-luh) *n.* a piece of land surrounded by water on three sides.

There are many **peninsulas** in Europe, including the Scandinavian, the Iberian, and the Italian peninsulas.

penny: (PEN-ee) *n.* a U.S. coin worth one cent.

Some people think finding a **penny** brings you good luck.

124

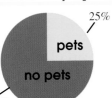

percent: (pur-SENT) *n.* a part of a whole expressed in parts of a hundred.

Only 25 **percent** of the students in my class have a pet.

perpendicular: (PUR-puhn-dik-yuh-lur) *adj.* lines or surfaces that meet at 90° angles.

These two red lines are **perpendicular**.

persuade: (puhr-SWAYD) *v.* to convince someone to do something or to believe something.

She **persuaded** her mother to let her go to the movies with her friends.

pharmacist: (FAR-muh-sist) *n.* a person whose job is to prepare and sell medicine.

Jodi got her medicine from the **pharmacist**.

piano: (pee-AN-oh) *n.* a musical instrument with white and black keys.

Frank is learning how to play the **piano**.

pie: (piy) *n.* a pastry filled with fruit, pudding, or other fillings.

We ate apple **pie** for dessert.

pig: (pig) *n.* a mammal with a long snout (nose) and hoofed feet.

The **pig** lives on the farm.

pilot: (PIY-lut) *n.* a person who operates an airplane.

The **pilot** landed the airplane at the airport.

125

Pp

piñata: (peen-YAH-tuh) *n.* a paper figure filled with toys or candy and used at celebrations.

All the children had a chance to hit the **piñata** at Manuel's birthday party.

pineapple: (PIYN-ap-ul) *n.* a fruit with a spiny outside and green leaves at the top.

The inside of the **pineapple** is juicy and delicious.

pink: (pingk) *adj.* a color.

This is the color **pink**.

1 cup   1 cup   1 pint

pint: (piynt) *n.* a unit of measurement equal to two cups.

We need a **pint** of milk to make the pancakes.

pioneer: (PIY-uh-neer) *n.* a person who is one of the first to settle a region.

Pioneers began moving to Kentucky in 1775.

plain: (playn) *n.* a large area of flat land.

The explorers traveled across the **plains**.

126

Elaine **planned** to decorate her house.

plan: (plan) *v.* to arrange an event ahead of time.

planet: (PLAN-ut) *n.* one of the nine large heavenly bodies that orbit around the sun.

The nine known **planets** in our solar system are Mercury, Venus, Earth, Mars, Jupiter, Saturn, Uranus, Neptune, and Pluto.

plant: (plant) *n.* any living thing that produces food from sunlight, such as grasses, trees, and flowers.

A **plant** needs sunlight and water to grow.

Dictionary Detective

The word *plain* has more than one meaning. Look up *plain* in a standard dictionary and find out the other meanings of this word. Choose one of these meanings and use it in a sentence.

plate: (playt) *n.* a shallow dish on which food is placed.

Please clear the last **plate** from the table.

plateau: (pla-TOH) *n.* a large, flat area of land that is higher than all the land around it.

The Desert Southwest region of North America has many **plateaus**.

play: (play) *n.* a story acted out on stage.

William Shakespeare performed many **plays** for Queen Elizabeth I.

playful: (PLAY-ful) *adj.* full of fun; merry.

Dean is being **playful** with his baby.

playground: (PLAY-grownd) *n.* an area used by children for outdoor play.

At recess, the children play on the **playground**.

pleasant: (PLEZ-unt) *adj.* pleasing or enjoyable.

It is a **pleasant** day for a picnic.

plenty: (PLEN-tee) *adj.* more than enough.

He has **plenty** of work to keep him busy.

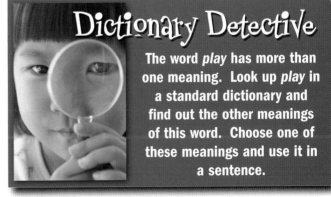

Dictionary Detective

The word *play* has more than one meaning. Look up *play* in a standard dictionary and find out the other meanings of this word. Choose one of these meanings and use it in a sentence.

Pp

---

plot: (plaht) *n.* the main story in a play or book.

The **plot** in William Shakespeare's play *Julius Caesar* centers around the murder of Caesar.

plumber: (PLUHM-ur) *n.* a person who fixes pipes, toilets, and other fixtures.

The **plumber** fixed the leak under the sink.

poetry: (POH-i-tree) *n.* writing that usually contains rhyme and rhythm.

> **STAR LIGHT, STAR BRIGHT**
>
> Star light, star bright,
> First star I see tonight.
> I wish I may,
> I wish I might,
> Have the wish I wish tonight.

In this example of **poetry**, the words *bright* and *tonight* rhyme.

point: (point) *v.* to direct a finger or other object toward something.

Roger **pointed** to his friends.

polar bear: (POH-lur bayr) *n.* a large mammal with white fur that lives in cold places.

The **polar bear** blends in with the color of the snow.

police car: (puh-LEES kahr) *n.* a vehicle used by a police officer.

The **police car** has a loud siren.

police officer: (puh-LEES AW-fi-sur) *n.* a person who makes sure people follow the law.

The **police officer** wrote down all the information about the car accident.

polite: (puh-LIYT) *adj.* showing good manners; being kind and thoughtful.

The **polite** girl helped the older woman across the street.

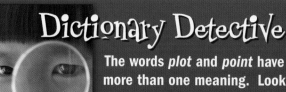

Dictionary Detective

The words *plot* and *point* have more than one meaning. Look up *plot* and *point* in a standard dictionary and find out the other meanings of these words. Choose one of these meanings and use it in a sentence.

politics: (PAHL-uh-tiks) *n.* the science and art of government.

Carl studied **politics** for years before he was elected mayor of his town.

pollution: (puh-LOO-shun) *n.* having harmful products in the environment.

pollution of our air or water could lead to serious health problems.

popcorn: (PAHP-kohrn) *n.* a snack food that comes from corn.

I like to eat **popcorn** when I go to the movies.

population: (pahp-yuh-LAY-shun) *n.* the total number of people who live in a specific area.

In 2000, the U.S. government counted the country's **population** and found that there were nearly 282 million people.

porch: (pohrch) *n.* a structure near the door to a house.

George left his shoes outside on the **porch**.

porcupine: (POHR-kyuh-piyn) *n.* a small mammal with stiff, sharp quills.

The **porcupine** uses its quills to protect itself from other animals.

potato: (puh-TAY-toh) *n.* a starchy vegetable that can be baked, boiled, or fried.

I like to eat a baked **potato** with my steak.

potato chip: (puh-TAY-toh chip) *n.* a thin slice of potato that is fried until crisp.

I ate a sandwich and **potato chips** for lunch.

Pp

pound: (pownd) *n.* a unit of weight equal to 16 ounces.

We bought a **pound** of coffee beans.

power: (POW-uhr) *n.* a force used to do work, such as electrical power.

This nuclear plant provides **power** for the entire city.

prehistoric: (pree-his-TOHR-ik) *adj.* related to the period of time before written history.

Woolly mammoths lived in **prehistoric** times.

prejudice: (PREJ-uh-dis) *n.* to like or dislike something without having a good reason.

In the 1800s, many Americans showed **prejudice** against the Irish immigrants.

present: 1. (PREZ-unt) *n.* the current time; right now. 2. (pri-ZENT) *v.* to bring before the public or identify something or someone.

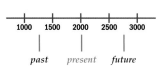

1. In history class we are discussing how past events helped shape the **present**.

2. Dr. Perna **presented** her ideas to the group.

president: (PREZ-uh-dunt) *n.* the leader of a modern republic or business.

George Washington was the first **president** of the United States.

pretend: (pri-TEND) *v.* to make believe.

Liam **pretended** to be a pirate.

pretty: (PRIT-ee) *adj.* pleasing to see or hear.

We watched a **pretty** sunset that turned the sky orange and red.

prime meridian: (priym muh-RID-ee-un) *n.* a line of longitude at 0 degrees that starts at the North Pole and passes through Greenwich, England to the South Pole.

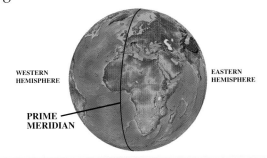

WESTERN HEMISPHERE

EASTERN HEMISPHERE

PRIME MERIDIAN

The **prime meridian** is the line of longitude from which all other longitude lines, east and west, are measured.

principal: (PRIN-suh-pul) *n.* the head or director of a school.

The **principal** announced that tomorrow is a school holiday.

produce: (pruh-DOOS) *v.* to make or manufacture.

In ancient Greece, people **produced** juice by crushing grapes with their feet.

product: (PRAHD-ukt) *n.* the result from multiplying two numbers together.

When you multiply five by six, the **product** is 30.

Selling Price	$7.00
Cost	$2.00
Profit	$5.00

profit: (PRAHF-it) *n.* the gain after all costs are subtracted from the selling price.

He made a $5 **profit** on each pen he sold.

propose: (pruh-POHZ) *v.* to suggest or offer something, such as an offer of marriage.

Jake was ready to get married and **proposed** to his girlfriend.

protect: (pruh-TEKT) *v.* to guard or keep safe.

The mother cat **protects** her kitten from harm.

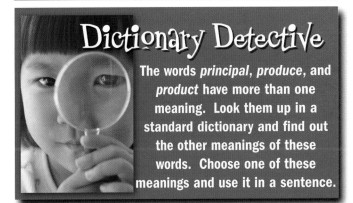

Dictionary Detective

The words *principal*, *produce*, and *product* have more than one meaning. Look them up in a standard dictionary and find out the other meanings of these words. Choose one of these meanings and use it in a sentence.

Pp

protest: (PROH-test) *v.* to object strongly to an idea or action.

Many people **protested** during the U.S. civil rights movement in the 1960s.

provoke: (pruh-VOHK) *v.* to cause to become angry.

If you **provoke** some insects, they might sting you.

pumpkin: (PUHMP-kin) *n.* a large, round orange fruit.

We carved the **pumpkin** for Halloween.

punctuation: (puhngk-choo-AY-shun) *n.* the system of using marks such as periods and commas to make writing clear.

It is important to have correct **punctuation** at the end of a sentence.

punish: (PUHN-ish) *v.* to make someone suffer for doing something wrong.

The teacher **punished** the boy for talking during class.

puppy: (PUHP-ee) *n.* a mammal; a young dog.

The **puppy** has a lot of energy.

purchase: (PUR-chis) *v.* to buy with money.

We **purchased** two tickets for the movie.

purple: (PUR-pul) *adj.* a color.

This is the color **purple**.

purse: (purs) *n.* a woman's handbag or pocketbook.

Mom put the car keys inside her **purse**.

quart: (kwohrt) *n.* a unit of measurement equal to two pints.

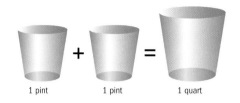

We needed a **quart** of water.

quarter: (KWOHR-tur) *n.* a U.S. coin worth 25 cents.

I need four **quarters** to buy a drink.

quarter past: (KWOHR-tur past) *n.* fifteen minutes after the hour.

We got home at **quarter past** seven.

quarter to (till): (KWOHR-tur too [(til)]) *n.* fifteen minutes before the hour.

He left work at **quarter to** five.

queen: (kween) *n.* a female leader or ruler.

Elizabeth I was a **queen** of England.

quiet: (KWIY-it) *adj.* making little or no sound.

If you are not **quiet**, you will wake the dog.

quotient: (KWOH-shunt) *n.* the result from dividing one number by another number.

When you divide 25 by five, the **quotient** is five.

Rr

rabbit: (RAB-it) *n.* a small mammal with long ears and a short tail.

John feeds his pet **rabbit** lettuce and carrots.

raccoon: (ra-KOON) *n.* a small mammal with a masklike stripe across its face and a bushy, ringed tail.

The **raccoon** looks for food at night.

racing car: (RAYS-ing kahr) *n.* an automobile used for competing in races.

This red **racing car** won the race.

radio: (RAY-dee-oh) *n.* a machine that plays music, news, and other broadcasts.

She listens to the **radio** in her bedroom.

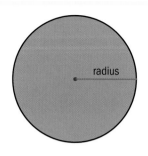

radius: (RAY-dee-us) *n.* a straight line extending from the center of a circle to its outer edge.

We learned how to calculate the **radius** of a circle.

railroad: (RAYL-rohd) *n.* a road made of steel rails on which a train travels.

Many Chinese immigrants helped build the first railroads in the United States.

rain: (rayn) *n.* water that falls in drops from clouds.

She used an umbrella to protect her from the **rain**.

raincoat: (RAYN-koht) *n.* a coat worn to protect a person from rain.

You'll need a **raincoat** if you go out in this storm.

ainfall: (RAYN-fawl) *n.* the amount of rain.

We had nine inches of **rainfall** last month.

raise: (rayz) *v.* to lift.

Ben **raised** his hand in class.

rake: (rayk) *n.* a tool for gathering cut grass or smoothing the ground.

We use the **rake** to clean up leaves that have fallen off the trees.

rat: (rat) *n.* a small mammal that looks like a mouse.

The **rat** ran into the street.

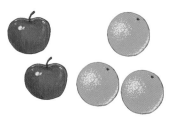

ratio: (RAY-shoh) *n.* the relationship in number between two things.

We have a **ratio** of two apples to three oranges.

reaction: (ree-AK-shun) *n.* a chemical change that happens when one substance affects another.

The **reaction** between metal and oxygen causes rust.

read: (reed) *v.* to understand language through written symbols.

Trenyce likes to **read** books in the library.

rebel: (ri-BEL) *v.* to fight against authority.

Some colonists **rebelled** against Great Britain by dumping tea in Boston Harbor.

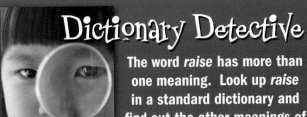

Dictionary Detective

The word *raise* has more than one meaning. Look up *raise* in a standard dictionary and find out the other meanings of this word. Choose one of these meanings and use it in a sentence.

Rr

recent: (REE-sunt) *adj.* relating to a time not long past.

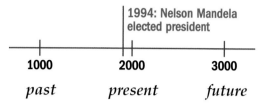

1994: Nelson Mandela elected president

| 1000 | 2000 | 3000 |
| past | present | future |

The election of President Nelson Mandela of South Africa is part of **recent** history.

recover: (ri-KUV-ur) *v.* to regain something, such as normal health.

She is **recovering** from the flu.

rectangle: (REK-tang-gul) *n.* a shape with four right angles in which the height is different from the width.

The room is in the shape of a **rectangle**.

recycle: (ree-SIY-kul) *v.* to take materials such as paper and cans and use them in another way.

This symbol shows people where they can **recycle** newspapers, empty soda cans, and other items.

136

---

red: (red) *adj.* a color.

This is the color **red**.

reduce: (ree-DOOS) *v.* to lessen or make smaller.

The total number of pennies has been **reduced** from five to two.

reference: (REF-runs) *n.* a book or other source of useful information.

I used the encyclopedia as a **reference** when I wrote my report.

reflect: (ri-FLEKT) *v.* to show an image as a mirror does.

The mirror **reflected** his face.

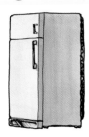

refrigerator: (ri-FRIJ-uh-ray-tur) *n.* a storage unit in the kitchen that uses electricity and keeps food cold.

I put the eggs and milk in the **refrigerator**.

refugee: (ref-yoo-JEE) *n.* a person who flees for safety.

These **refugees** left Ethiopia, a country in Africa, to find a safer place to live.

region: (REE-jun) *n.* an area of land that has the same kind of weather, plant and animal life, or other things in common.

The **region** we call the American Southwest is made up of the states of Arizona, New Mexico, Oklahoma, and Texas.

relationship: (ri-LAY-shuhn-ship) *n.* the state of being related or connected.

Mr. and Mrs. Martinez have a loving **relationship**.

relax: (ri-LAKS) *v.* to rest.

Brian likes to **relax** after work.

religion: (ri-LIJ-un) *n.* a set of beliefs and practices concerning God or the supernatural.

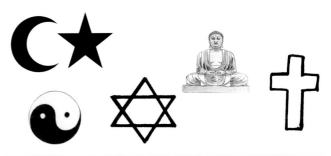

There are many different **religions** in the world.

repair: (ri-PAYR) *v.* to fix.

The custodian **repaired** the broken drinking fountain.

Teacher says:
"I pledge allegiance to the flag ..."

Class repeats:
"I pledge allegiance to the flag ..."

repeat: (ri-PEET) *v.* to say or do again.

To teach us the pledge of allegiance, the teacher asked us to **repeat** the words after him.

137

Rr

representative: (rep-ri-ZEN-tuh-tiv) *n.* a person chosen to do something or make decisions for other people.

In the United States, the **representatives** in Congress make laws for people to follow.

reptile: (REP-tiyl) *n.* a cold-blooded vertebrate (animal with a backbone) that has skin covered in scales.

Snakes and lizards are examples of **reptiles**.

republic: (ri-PUHB-lik) *n.* a government in which the citizens vote for representatives to lead the government.

France is one of many countries in Europe that is a **republic**.

reputation: (rep-yuh-TAY-shun) *n.* the overall character of a person as judged by people in general.

Spaniard Francisco Pizarro had a **reputation** for being cruel to the people of the Inca empire.

rescue: (RES-kyoo) *v.* to free from danger; save.

The firefighters **rescued** everyone from the burning building.

research: (REE-surch) *v.* to study carefully in order to discover new knowledge.

Ricky **researched** how electrical power is produced.

resources: (REE-sohr-sez) *n.* usable supplies or wealth.

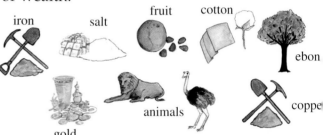

These are some of the many natural **resources** found in Africa.

respond: (ri-SPAHND) *v.* to act in response; react.

The ambulance workers **responded** to the call for help.

responsibility: (ri-spahn-suh-BIL-uh-tee) *n.* something that someone is trusted or expected to do.

It is Antonio's **responsibility** to wash the dog.

138

evolution: (rev-uh-LOO-shun) *n.* a sudden overthrow of the government by the people who are being governed.

The monarchy in France ended with the French **Revolution**.

LOST DOG

Reward: $100

reward: (ri-WAWRD) *n.* money or another prize given to someone for doing something.

He is offering a **reward** of $100 to anyone who finds his lost dog.

rhinoceros: (riy-NAHS-ur-us) *n.* a large mammal with thick skin and one or two horns on its nose.

The **rhinoceros** may get angry if it thinks it is in danger.

rhyme: (riym) *v.* to end with a similar sound.

The Raven
by Edgar Allen Poe
Once upon a midnight dreary
while I pondered, weak and weary ...

The words *dreary* and *weary* **rhyme**.

rice: (riys) *n.* a starchy grain used for food.

Sarah's family eats **rice** with most meals.

right: (riyt) *adj.* located on the side of the body away from the heart.

Right

Julio looked to the **right**.

ring: (ring) *n.* an item of jewelry worn on the finger.

Elizabeth began wearing this **ring** when Richard asked her to marry him.

ritual: (RICH-oo-ul) *n.* a ceremony or action performed the same way over time.

The exchange of rings during a wedding ceremony is a **ritual** in many cultures.

Dictionary Detective

The word *revolution* has more than one meaning. Look up *revolution* in a standard dictionary and find out the other meanings of this word. Choose one of these meanings and use it in a sentence.

river: (RIV-ur) *n.* a large stream of water.

Steven took his boat down the **river**.

road: (rohd) *n.* a flat surface on which cars and people travel.

This **road** leads to the Smiths' farm.

robe: (rohb) *n.* loose clothing worn in the house.

This **robe** keeps me warm after I shower.

rock: (rahk) *n.* stone; a very hard mineral.

The family stopped to look at the large **rock**.

rocket: (RAHK-it) *n.* a tubelike vehicle that flies into outer space; a rocket can be used only once.

The **rocket** flew to the moon.

roller skate: (ROHL-ur skayt) *n.* a shoe with four wheels on the bottom.

I can't go skating in the park until I find my other **roller skate**.

Roman
numeral
five

Roman numeral: (ROH-man NOO-muhr-ul) *n.* a numeral in the ancient Roman system: I, V, X, L, C, D, and M.

The **Roman numeral** for five is V.

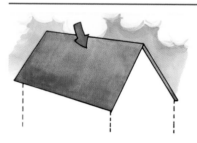

roof: (roof) *n.* the covering on the top of a building.

The **roof** keeps rain and snow from coming into the house.

Take the "r" off the word *rock* and replace it with an "l." What word do you get? Now replace it with an "s." What word does that make? Use both of these new words in a sentence.

room: (room) *n.* a part of a building or house with walls and a doorway.

The class meets every afternoon in this **room**.

rooster: (ROOS-tur) *n.* a bird; a male chicken.

The **rooster** crows in the morning.

rotate: (ROH-tayt) *v.* to turn in circles.

The earth **rotates** toward the east.

rough: (ruhf) *adj.* uneven in surface; rugged or harsh.

The **rough** road is difficult to drive on.

route: (root) *n.* a course of travel; a way.

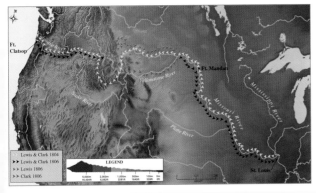

Explorers Lewis and Clark took different **routes** when they returned to the East.

routine: (roo-TEEN) *n.* a usual way of doing something.

Part of Halley's nightly **routine** is brushing her teeth.

ruins: (ROO-ins) *n.* the remains of something that has been destroyed.

We can learn about ancient Roman culture by studying Roman **ruins**.

ruler: (ROO-lur) *n.* a strip of wood or other material with a straight edge used for measuring inches or centimeters.

Use your **ruler** to measure the width of your desk.

run: (ruhn) *n.* to move faster than a walk.

Linda **runs** five miles every day.

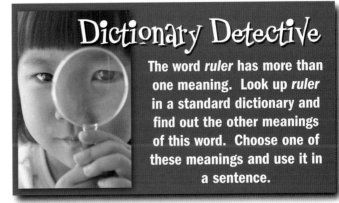

Dictionary Detective

The word *ruler* has more than one meaning. Look up *ruler* in a standard dictionary and find out the other meanings of this word. Choose one of these meanings and use it in a sentence.

sacred: (SAY-krid) *adj.* holy.

Torah

Bible

Qur'an

The **sacred** books of Judaism, Christianity, and Islam are the Torah, Bible, and Qur'an, respectively.

sacrifice: (SAK-ruh-fiys) *n.* the act of giving up something enjoyable.

Not eating dessert was a **sacrifice**, but Bob really wanted to lose weight.

sad: (sad) *adj.* filled with unhappiness or sorrow.

Alicia felt **sad** when she broke her toy.

sailboat: (SAYL-boht) *n.* a boat that has a piece of cloth (the sail) to catch the wind and move it forward.

The **sailboat** moved across the ocean.

salad: (SAL-ud) *n.* a cold dish of vegetables, such as lettuce, tomatoes, and cucumbers.

Many people eat **salad** before their main meal.

sales clerk: (saylz klurk) *n.* a person who sells goods in a store.

The **sales clerk** sold Rita a dress.

salt: (sahlt) *n.* a mineral used to add flavor to food and keep it fresh.

I like to add **salt** to my popcorn.

ame: (saym) *adj.* very much alike.

The twins look the **same**.

andbox: (SAND-bahks) *n.* a box filled with and that children can play in.

The children left a small red shovel in the **sandbox**.

 **sandwich:** (SAND-wich) *n.* two slices of bread with layers of meat, cheese, or other fillings between them.

I brought a **sandwich** for lunch.

satisfy: (SAT-is-fiy) *v.* to meet the needs of.

The watermelon **satisfied** her hunger.

 **Saturday:** (SAT-ur-day) *n.* the day of the week after Friday and before Sunday.

Our soccer team plays on **Saturday** mornings.

 **saw:** (saw) *n.* a tool with a metal blade used for cutting.

Daniel used the **saw** to cut wood.

 **scare:** (skayr) *v.* to frighten; to make afraid.

The movie about ghosts **scared** her.

school bus: (skool buhs) *n.* a long vehicle with many seats used to bring students to and from school.

Julio and Ron ride the **school bus** together.

science: (SIY-uns) *n.* the study of humans, animals, plants, and the world.

Chemistry, biology, and physics are areas of **science**.

 **scissors:** (SIZ-urz) *n.* a sharp tool used to cut paper and other materials.

We need **scissors** and yarn for the art project.

 **scream:** (skreem) *v.* to cry out with a loud sound.

The children **screamed** with excitement as they celebrated the new year.

sea: (see) *n.* a large body of salt water partially surrounded by land.

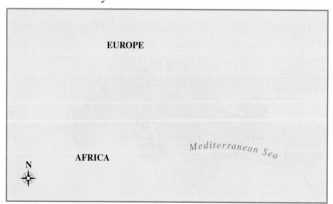

EUROPE

AFRICA

Mediterranean Sea

N

The Mediterranean **Sea** is north of Africa.

 **sea horse:** (SEE hohrs) *n.* a small fish with a long tail and snout (nose and mouth).

The **sea horse** uses its tail to hold onto underwater plants.

 **sea turtle:** (see TURT-ul) *n.* a reptile; a large turtle that swims.

The divers saw a **sea turtle** in the ocean.

 **seal:** (seel) *n.* a mamma with flippers (feet for swimming).

The **seal** rested on the rocks near the shore.

 **search:** (surch) *v.* to look carefully to try to find something.

Mr. Watson used a flashlight to **search** for his lost keys.

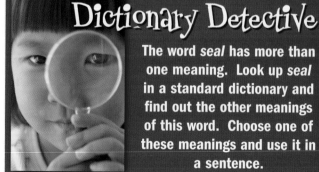

Dictionary Detective

The word *seal* has more than one meaning. Look up *seal* in a standard dictionary and find out the other meanings of this word. Choose one of these meanings and use it in a sentence.

season: (SEE-zun) *n.* one of the four parts of the year.

Winter

Spring

Summer

Fall

The four **seasons** are winter, spring, summer, and fall.

second: (SEK-und) *adj.* next after the first.

The **second** owl landed on the tree branch.

secretary: (SEK-ruh-tayr-ee) *n.* a person responsible for office work such as keeping records, sending letters, and answering telephones.

The **secretary** is taking phone messages for her boss.

security: (si-KYOOR-uh-tee) *n.* the state of being safe.

I use this lock on my bike for extra **security**.

seed: (seed) *n.* a small part of a plant that grows into a new plant.

A watermelon has hundreds of **seeds**.

September: (sep-TEM-bur) *n.* the ninth month of the year.

Many schools start a new year in **September**.

sequence: (see-kwuns) *n.* the following of one thing after another.

ABCDEFG

The letters in the English alphabet follow a certain **sequence**.

set: (set) *v.* to put something in a particular place.

Rene **set** the plates on the table.

Ss

setting: (SET-ing) *n.* the location or environment in which something takes place.

Japan is the **setting** for the book *The Tale of Genji*.

seven: (SEV-un) *n.* a number equaling six plus one; numbers are usually used as adjectives in a sentence.

Thomas played with **seven** tops.

seventeen: (sev-un-TEEN) *n.* a number equaling 10 plus seven; numbers are usually used as adjectives in a sentence.

Seventeen butterflies flew across the field.

seventh: (SEV-unth) *adj.* next after sixth.

The **seventh** owl landed on the tree branch.

seventy: (SEV-un-tee) *n.* a number equaling 10 times seven; numbers are usually used as adjectives in a sentence.

70

Ten rows of seven dots make a total of **seventy** dots.

several: (SEV-ur-ul) *adj.* more than two, but fewer than many in number.

The student brought **several** pencils to class to share with his study group.

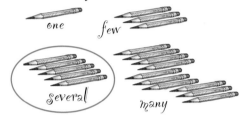 **sewing machine:** (SOH-ing muh-SHEEN) *n.* a machine for stitching material.

Beth used the **sewing machine** to shorten her skirt

shallow: (SHAL-oh) *adj.* not deep.

The water in the children's pool is **shallow**.

share: (shayr) *v.* to give part of something to another person.

Sandy and Jordan **shared** an ice-cream cone.

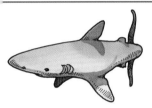 **shark:** (shahrk) *n.* a large fish; sharks come in many different shapes and sizes.

Some **sharks** can be dangerous.

 **sharp:** (shahrp) *adj.* having a cutting edge or sharp point.

We need **sharp** scissors to cut through this paper.

 **sheep:** (sheep) *n.* a mammal with white wool (thick hair) and hooves.

Wool comes from **sheep**.

 **shell:** (shel) *n.* a hard outer covering.

I found a **shell** on the beach.

shelter: (SHEL-tur) *n.* something that covers or protects.

The tent gave us **shelter** from the rain.

 **ship:** (ship) *n.* a large boat used for traveling on the ocean.

The **ship** traveled around the world.

 **shirt:** (shurt) *n.* a garment for the upper part of the body.

It is a good idea to wear a long-sleeved **shirt** when the weather is cold.

shoe: (shoo) *n.* a foot covering.

Shoes keep your feet warm and protected.

---

short: (shohrt) *adj.* not tall or long.

Sheila is **short** compared to her tall friend.

shorts: (shohrts) *n.* a covering for the top part of the legs that is shorter than pants.

Martin likes to wear **shorts** during the summer.

---

shoulder: (SHOHL-dur) *n.* the part of the body where the arm joins the rest of the body.

You can hurt your **shoulder** if your book bag is too heavy.

shovel: (SHUHV-ul) *n.* a tool consisting of a blade or scoop and a long handle.

Kelly dug a hole with a **shovel**.

---

show: (shoh) *v.* to place in sight; display.

Kenny **shows** the class his ant colony.

---

sick: (sik) *adj.* having ill health; not feeling well.

Kurt is **sick** with the flu.

---

sidewalk: (SIYD-wawk) *n.* a paved walkway alongside a road.

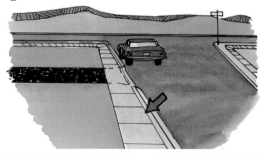

Cara walked to school on the **sidewalk**.

sideways: (SIYD-wayz) *adj.* moving or facing to one side.

Crabs walk **sideways**.

simile: (SIM-uh-lee) *n.* a figure of speech comparing two unlike things using *like* or *as*.

Using **similes** such as, "Your lips are like rubies," can make your writing more interesting.

sink: (singk) *n.* a basin used for washing.

She washed her hands in the **sink**.

sister: (SIS-tur) *n.* a female relative who has the same parents as another person.

Tina likes holding her little **sister**.

sit: (sit) *v.* to be seated.

Will and his grandpa like to **sit** next to each other.

six: (siks) *n.* a number equaling five plus one; numbers are usually used as adjectives in a sentence.

Susan picked **six** strawberries.

sixteen: (sik-STEEN) *n.* a number equaling 10 plus six; numbers are usually used as adjectives in a sentence.

Sixteen flies flew over the garbage.

sixth: (siksth) *adj.* the next after fifth.

The **sixth** owl landed on the tree branch.

Ss

sixty: (SIK-stee) *n.* a number equaling 10 times six; numbers are usually used as adjectives in a sentence.

Ten rows of six dots make a total of **sixty** dots.

skateboard: (SKAYT-bohrd) *n.* a board on wheels.

Coby practices riding his **skateboard** in the driveway.

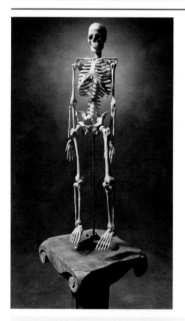

skeleton: (SKEL-uh-tun) *n.* the hard frame of a body made up of bones.

The adult human **skeleton** has 206 bones.

skin: (skin) *n.* the soft covering of the body.

Nikki's **skin** gets burned if she stays in the sun too long.

skirt: (skurt) *n.* clothing that hangs from the waist and is not attached between the legs.

She wore a green **skirt** to the dance.

skunk: (skuhnk) *n.* a mammal with a bushy tail and black and white fur.

A **skunk** will make a terrible smell if you frighten it.

sky: (skiy) *n.* the region of air over the earth.

The **sky** is clear and blue today.

slavery: (SLAY-vuh-ree) *n.* the practice of owning a person and forcing him or her to work for free.

Slavery in the United States did not end until after the U.S. Civil War.

sleepy: (SLEE-pee) *adj.* tired; drowsy.

Marcia feels **sleepy** if she stays up too late.

slender: (SLEN-dur) *adj.* long and thin; not wide.

These trees are tall and **slender**.

slide: (sliyd) *n.* playground equipment consisting of a ladder and a sloped surface.

Billy went up and down the **slide** all afternoon.

slipper: (SLIP-ur) *n.* a light shoe worn inside.

John likes to wear **slippers** around the house.

slow: (sloh) *adj.* moving at less than usual speed.

Turtles are **slow**.

small: (smahl) *adj.* little in size.

Most insects are **small**.

smart: (smahrt) *adj.* quick to learn; bright.

She must be very **smart** to get such good grades.

smog: (smawg) *n.* fog containing smoke or other pollution.

Pollution from cars adds to the **smog** over the city.

smooth: (smooth) *adj.* having an even surface; not rough.

Silk is a **smooth** type of cloth.

Ss

snail: (snayl) *n.* a slow-moving invertebrate (animal with no backbone) with a shell.

The **snail** ate the plants in our garden.

snake: (snayk) *n.* a long reptile that has no legs.

Stan was afraid of being bitten by the **snake**.

snow: (snoh) *n.* small crystals of ice that fall from the sky.

Martin pulled his sled through the **snow**.

soap: (sohp) *n.* a substance used for washing and cleaning.

The mother washed the baby with **soap**.

soccer ball: (SAHK-ur bawl) *n.* a medium-sized ball, often black and white, used to play soccer.

He kicked the **soccer ball** into the goal.

sock: (sahk) *n.* a soft material used to cover the foot.

People wear **socks** to keep their feet warm.

soda: (SOH-duh) *n.* a drink with bubbles.

Sam bought a can of **soda**.

sofa: (SOH-fuh) *n.* a couch; a soft place where people can sit.

We sat on the **sofa** and watched television.

soft: (sawft) *adj.* smooth or delicate to the touch.

The rabbit's fur is **soft**.

soil: (soil) *n.* the loose surface material of the earth.

We planted vegetable seeds in the **soil**.

solar system: (SOH-lur SIS-tum) *n.* the sun and planets, meteors, and other objects that move around the sun.

Our **solar system** has nine planets.

soldier: (SOHL-jur) *n.* a person who defends and fights for a country or other organized group.

Paul is a **soldier** in the U.S. Army.

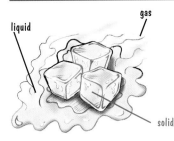

liquid gas

solid

solid: (SAHL-id) *n.* hard; neither liquid nor gas.

Ice is the **solid** form of water.

solution: (suh-LOO-shun) *n.* the answer to a problem.

The father offered a **solution** to the disagreement between the two children.

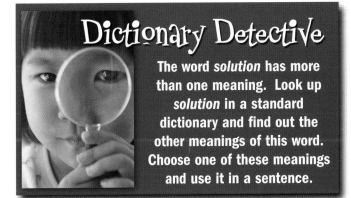

Dictionary Detective

The word *solution* has more than one meaning. Look up *solution* in a standard dictionary and find out the other meanings of this word. Choose one of these meanings and use it in a sentence.

153

Ss

song: (sawng) *n.* vocal music.

Families sing a special **song** as they go from house to house on Las Posadas.

sorrow: (SAHR-oh) *n.* deep sadness; grief.

We felt **sorrow** when Uncle Milo died.

soup: (soop) *n.* a liquid food made by cooking vegetables, seasonings, and sometimes meat or fish.

Hot **soup** makes a great meal on a cold day.

sour: (sowr) *adj.* having an acid taste.

Lemons taste **sour**.

154

south: (sowth) *n.* the direction opposite of north

On most maps, **south** is toward the bottom.

space: (spays) *n.* the region beyond the earth's atmosphere.

Astronauts need special equipment to travel in **space**.

space capsule: (spays KAP-sul) *n.* a sealed cabin or vehicle in which a person or animal can travel in space.

The astronaut circled the earth in a **space capsule**

space shuttle: (spays SHUHT-ul) *n.* a spacecraft that takes people into outer space and then back; a space shuttle can land and be reused.

Astronauts conduct many experiments while aboard the **space shuttle**.

spaghetti: (spuh-GET-ee) *n.* a food made from flour, eggs, and water that is cut into long strings and dried; pasta.

or dinner we had **spaghetti** and meatballs.

speak: (speek) *v.* to talk.

anya **speaks** to her friend on the phone every day.

spectacular: (spek-TAK-yuh-lur) *adj.* striking; thrilling.

he circus performers put on a **spectacular** show.

speech: (speech) *n.* a public talk.

Dr. Martin Luther King, Jr. gave many famous peeches, including his "I have a dream" speech.

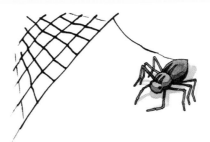

spider: (SPIY-dur) *n.* a small animal with eight legs.

The **spider** made a web in the corner of the room.

spinach: (SPIN-ich) *n.* a green, leafy vegetable.

Laura likes to eat cooked **spinach**.

---

sponge: (spuhnj) *n.* a material that absorbs water and is used for cleaning.

He used the **sponge** to wash the dishes.

---

spoon: (spoon) *n.* a tool for eating and stirring.

He stirred his coffee with a **spoon**.

Ss

spring: (spring) *n.* the season between winter and summer.

Many birds and other animals are born during the **spring**.

square: (skwayr) *n.* a shape that has four right angles and four sides of the same length.

Liz drew an orange **square** on her paper.

squirrel: (skwurl) *n.* a small mammal with a bushy tail.

The **squirrel** ate the bread people left behind in the park.

stairs: (stayrz) *n.* a series of steps.

The **stairs** lead from the hallway to the basement.

stand: (stand) *v.* to be on one's feet.

I will **stand** in line and wait for my turn.

stanza: (STAN-zuh) *n.* a group of lines in a poem.

> Shall I compare thee to a summer's day?
> Thou art more lovely and more temperate:
> Rough winds do shake the darling buds of May,
> And summer's lease hath all too short a date:
> Sometime too hot the eye of heaven shines,
> And often is his gold complexion dimm'd;

stanza one

> And every fair from fair sometime declines,
> By chance, or nature's changing course untrimm'd;
> But thy eternal summer shall not fade,
> Nor lose possession of that fair thou ow'st;
> Nor shall Death brag thou wander'st in his shade,
> When in eternal lines to time thou grow'st:

stanza two

> So long as man can breath, or eyes can see,
> So long lives this, and this gives life to thee.

stanza three

The first **stanza** of this poem by William Shakespeare is about a woman's beauty.

star: (stahr) *n.* a figure having five or six points around a center

The teacher put a **star** on his test because he got all the answers correct.

Dictionary Detective

The words *spring* and *star* have more than one meaning. Look them up in a standard dictionary and find out the other meanings of these words. Choose one of these meanings and use it in a sentence.

156

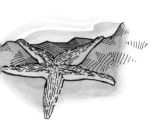

starfish: (STAHR-fish) *n.* a fish that is shaped like a star.

We found a **starfish** on the beach.

station wagon: (STAY-shun WAG-un) *n.* an automobile that has an area behind the seats for suitcases and other items.

We drive in the **station wagon** when we go on vacation.

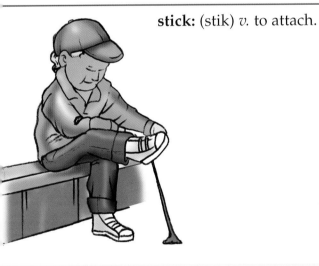

stick: (stik) *v.* to attach.

The gum is **sticking** to his shoe.

stomach: (STUHM-uk) *n.* the part of the body below the chest.

The little boy splashed water on his **stomach**.

stop: (stahp) *v.* to no longer move; to come to an end.

This sign tells cars to **stop**.

storm: (stohrm) *n.* heavy rainfall or snowfall, often with strong winds.

The **storm** brought a lot of rain and wind.

stove: (stohv) *n.* something that provides heat for cooking.

Lee cooked dinner on the **stove**.

strawberry: (STRAW-bayr-ee) *n.* a sweet, red fruit with many tiny seeds.

I ate the last **strawberry** with my breakfast.

Sounds Like Fun!

Take the word *straw* out of *strawberry*. What word do you end up with?

Ss

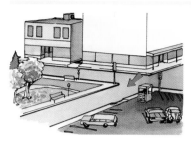

street: (street) *n.* a paved roadway.

The bank is located down the **street**.

stretch: (strech) *v.* to extend or spread out.

She **stretched** her arms out wide.

strike: (striyk) *n.* when people stop working to force their employer to agree to demands.

The workers are on **strike** because they want better pay.

strong: (strahng) *adj.* having great power.

Darlene must be **strong** to lift those heavy weights.

submarine: (SUHB-muh-reen) *n.* a boat that can travel under water.

The people in the **submarine** saw many different kinds of fish.

20−15=5

subtraction: (SUHB-trak-shun) *n.* the act o finding the difference between two numbers

Using **subtraction** we know that 20 minus 15 equals five.

succeed: (suk-SEED) *v.* to do well.

You must study hard to **succeed** in school.

suggest: (suhg-JEST) *v.* to offer an idea.

Caitlin **suggested** that Mr. Lee build a new room in his house.

158

suit: (soot) *n.* two or three pieces of clothing designed to be worn together.

Nathan wore a **suit** to work every day.

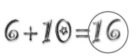

sum: (suhm) *n.* the result of adding two numbers together.

The **sum** of six and 10 is 16.

summary: (SUHM-uh-ree) *n.* a brief statement that includes the main point of something.

The magazine printed **summaries** of the new books.

summer: (SUHM-ur) *n.* the season between spring and fall.

Many people visit the beach during the **summer**.

Sunday: (SUHN-day) *n.* the day of the week after Saturday and before Monday.

The Sanchez family goes out to breakfast every **Sunday**.

sunny: (SUHN-ee) *adj.* full of sunshine.

We like to go to the park on **sunny** days.

supervise: (SOO-pur-viyz) *v.* to watch over.

The lifeguard **supervises** the people swimming in the ocean.

supply and demand: (suh-PLIY and di-MAND) *n.* the economic idea that the price of a product depends on the level of supply and demand for the product.

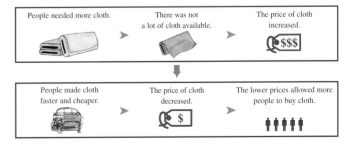

This chart shows how **supply and demand** affects the price of cloth.

159

Ss

Income
$12,000
Bills
$10,000
Surplus
$2,000

surplus: (SUR-plus) *n.* an extra amount left over.

We had a **surplus** of $2,000 after paying our bills.

surprised: (sur-PRIYZD) *adj.* to feel amazement because something is unexpected.

She was **surprised** by the gift.

surrender: (suh-REN-dur) *v.* to give up, especially after force is used.

General Robert E. Lee **surrendered** to General Ulysses S. Grant, ending the Civil War in the United States.

surround: (suh-ROWND) *v.* to be on all sides.

The baby was **surrounded** by pumpkins.

WANTED—
Suspect in a Crime

Call the police
if you see this man.

suspect: (SUHS-pekt) *n.* a person who is thought to have done something—usually something wrong.

The police searched for the **suspect**.

suspicious: (suh-SPISH-us) *adj.* causing a lack of trust.

Airport workers look for anything odd or **suspicious** in travelers' bags.

swamp: (swahmp) *n.* wet, spongy land, often containing a great deal of plant life.

Alligators and mosquitoes live in **swamps**.

sweater: (SWET-ur) *n.* a knitted covering for the upper body.

This pink **sweater** will keep you warm.

sweet: (sweet) *adj.* tasting of sugar.

Pies, cakes, and many other desserts are **sweet**.

sweet potato: (sweet puh-TAY-toh) *n.* a thick vegetable with brown skin.

Suzanna makes a pie out of **sweet potatoes** and spices.

swing: (swing) *n.* playground equipment with a seat hanging from two chains.

The children were happy to see the two new **swings** on the playground.

symbol: (SIM-bul) *n.* something that represents something else; a sign.

The white dove is a **symbol** of peace.

symbolism: (SIM-buh-liz-um) *n.* the practice of expressing meaning through the use of symbols.

From Robert Frost's

"The Road Not Taken"

. . . I shall be telling this with a sigh
Somewhere ages and ages hence:
Two roads diverged in a wood, and I—
I took the one less traveled by,
And that has made all the difference.

This poem uses **symbolism** to show how making life choices is like traveling down a path.

synonym: (SIN-uh-nim) *n.* a word having the same or nearly the same meaning as another word in the same language.

Ill and *sick* are **synonyms**.

table: (TAY-bul) *n.* a piece of furniture that has a flat surface and one or more legs for support.

We got a new kitchen **table**.

taco: (TAH-koh) *n.* a cooked tortilla (flat bread) folded over and filled with meat, tomatoes, lettuce, and cheese.

They served **tacos** in the cafeteria.

tall: (tawl) *adj.* having great height.

Katherine is **tall** compared to her friend.

tame: (taym) *adj.* no longer wild; friendly to people.

The circus lion is **tame** and follows the trainer's commands.

tape player: (tayp PLAY-ur) *n.* a machine for playing taped recordings of music, speech, or other sounds.

Our teacher played music on the **tape player**.

taste: (tayst) *v.* to sample a food.

The puppy **tasted** the ice cream.

Paycheck	
Salary	$1200.00
Federal Tax	-$205.34
State Tax	-$49.57
Net Pay	**$945.09**

tax: (taks) *n.* money that people and businesses pay to the government for public use.

The state **taxes** will help pay for the new roads.

teacher: (TEE-chur) *n.* a person who instruct students.

Meg's **teacher** helped her with the math problem.

teapot: (TEE-paht) *n.* a container in which tea is made.

Mr. Wang used the **teapot** to make tea.

telephone: (TEL-uh-fohn) *n.* a small machine used for talking and listening from a distance.

Ashley called her grandmother on the **telephone**.

telescope: (TEL-uh-skohp) *n.* an instrument with lenses that make it possible to see objects that are far away.

We looked at the stars and planets through a **telescope**.

television: (TEL-uh-vizh-un) *n.* a machine with a screen that shows moving images.

We watch the news on **television** each night.

temperature: (TEM-pur-uh-chur) *n.* a measurement of warmth or coldness.

The **temperature** today is hot.

ten: (ten) *n.* a number equaling nine plus one; numbers are usually used as adjectives in a sentence.

10

Two rows of five dots make a total of **ten** dots.

tenth: (tenth) *adj.* the next after ninth.

The **tenth** owl landed on the tree branch.

terrarium: (tuh-RAYR-ee-um) *n.* a glass container used for keeping plants or small animals.

The plant in the **terrarium** needs water.

163

territory: (TAYR-uh-tohr-ee) *n.* a large area of land.

The United States bought the **territory** shown in purple from France; this agreement was called the Louisiana Purchase.

textile: (TEKS-tiyl) *n.* a woven or knit cloth.

Before machines were invented to produce cloth more quickly, all **textiles** were made by hand.

theme: (theem) *n.* the overall idea expressed in a written work.

The **theme** of this book is that if you are lost in a store, you should ask someone who works there for help.

theory: (THEER-ee) *n.* a general rule that explains known facts or experiences.

The student had a **theory** that if he studied all the vocabulary words from the chapter, he would do well on the test.

thermometer: (THUR-mahm-uh-tur) *n.* an instrument for measuring temperature.

The mother used a **thermometer** to take her son's temperature when he was sick.

thick: (thik) *adj.* having great size from one surface to the opposite surface.

It was difficult to cut through the **thick** tree.

thin: (thin) *adj.* having little size from one surface to the opposite surface; slim.

thin →   ← fat

The **thin** cat should eat a little more.

third: (thurd) *adj.* the next after second.

The **third** owl landed on the branch.

thirsty: (THUR-stee) *adj.* needing liquid.

He felt **thirsty** after running the race.

thirteen: (thur-TEEN) *n.* a number equaling 10 plus three; numbers are usually used as adjectives in a sentence.

13

The classroom has **thirteen** erasers.

thirty: (THUR-tee) *n.* a number equaling 10 times three; numbers are usually used as adjectives in a sentence.

30

Five rows of six dots make a total of **thirty** dots.

three: (three) *n.* a number equaling two plus one; numbers are usually used as adjectives in a sentence.

3

These **three** chicks are looking for food.

through: (throo) *prep.* in at one side and out the other.

He drove **through** the tunnel in the mountain.

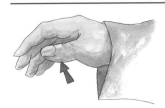 **thumb:** (thuhm) *n.* the short, thick digit on each hand.

He hurt his **thumb** when he caught the baseball.

 **Thursday:** (THURZ-day) *n.* the day of the week after Wednesday and before Friday.

Marta has piano lessons every **Thursday**.

 **ticket:** (TIK-it) *n.* a slip of paper showing a person has paid to enter a place or for some other service.

I bought a **ticket** to see the movie.

tiger: (TIY-gur) *n.* a large, striped mammal; a wild cat.

The **tiger** attacks other animals.

tiny: (TIY-nee) *adj.* very small.

She needed a magnifying glass to see the **tiny** insects.

tired: (tiyrd) *adj.* to feel the need for sleep.

The **tired** woman was ready to go to bed.

tissue: (TISH-oo) *n.* a soft paper used for purposes such as clearing the nose.

You should cover your nose with a **tissue** when you sneeze.

to: (too) *prep.* directed toward.

Marco gave this gift **to** Sara.

toast: (tohst) *n.* sliced bread that has been browned by heat.

He eats **toast** with butter in the morning.

Sunday	
Monday	
Tuesday	yesterday
Wednesday	today
Thursday	tomorrow
Friday	
Saturday	

today: (tuh-DAY) *n.* this day.

Today is my birthday.

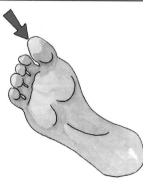

toe: (toh) *n.* one of the five digits on the end of the foot.

She hurt her **toe** when she fell.

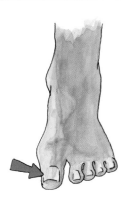

toenail: (TOH-nayl) *n.* the hard covering at the end of the toe.

He keeps his **toenails** cut short.

toilet: (TOI-lit) *n.* a bathroom fixture used for getting rid of bodily waste.

Dad uses bleach and a brush to clean the **toilet.**

tomato: (tuh-MAY-toh) *n.* a large, juicy fruit that can be eaten raw or cooked.

I like slices of **tomato** on my sandwiches.

tomorrow: (tuh-MAHR-oh) *n.* the day after today.

Sunday	
Monday	
Tuesday	yesterday
Wednesday	today
Thursday	(tomorrow)
Friday	
Saturday	

We're going on a class field trip **tomorrow.**

tongue: (tuhng) *n.* the part of the body inside the mouth used for tasting.

The doctor asked Maggie to stick out her **tongue.**

tool: (tool) *n.* something used to do a particular job.

Joan needed several **tools** to fix her sink.

tooth: (tooth) *n.* the part of the mouth used for chewing.

The dentist fixed Pam's broken **tooth.**

toothbrush: (TOOTH-bruhsh) *n.* a small brush with a long handle used for brushing teeth.

The dentist gave Carlos a new **toothbrush.**

167

Tt

toothpaste: (TOOTH-payst) *n.* a substance used to clean teeth.

He likes to brush his teeth with mint-flavored **toothpaste**.

top: (tahp) *adj.* the highest part of something.

The man had pigeons on the **top** of his head.

total: (TOHT-ul) *n.* making up the whole.

I had two pencils and Rosa had five pencils, for a **total** of seven pencils.

tough: (tuhf) *adj.* strong.

The **tough** dog scared the small child.

tow truck: (toh truk) *n.* a vehicle used to move another vehicle.

We called a **tow truck** when our car broke.

toward: (twahrd) *prep.* in the direction of.

The ballplayer ran **toward** second base.

towel: (TOW-ul) *n.* a cloth used to dry the hands, face, or body.

Gilberto used a **towel** to dry off after swimming.

tower: (TOW-ur) *n.* a very high building.

The Eiffel **Tower** is located in Paris, France.

trade: (trayd) *v.* to buy and sell; to exchange.

These American Indians are **trading** corn for animal skins.

tradition: (truh-DISH-un) *n.* a custom handed down from one generation to another.

It is a **tradition** in the United States to watch fireworks on July 4th.

tragedy: (TRAJ-uh-dee) *n.* a serious play that has a sad ending.

The play *Romeo and Juliet* is a famous **tragedy** in which a young boy and girl die.

trailer: (TRAY-lur) *n.* a large wagon pulled by a vehicle.

We use our **trailer** to bring home large items.

train: (trayn) *n.* a connected group of railroad cars pulled or pushed by an engine.

We rode the **train** from San Francisco to San Diego.

transportation: (trans-pur-TAY-shun) *n.* the act of carrying something, such as a person, from one place to another.

The subway is one form of **transportation**.

trash can: (trash kan) *n.* a container for garbage.

She put all the garbage in the **trash can**.

trash collector: (trash kuh-LEK-tur) *n.* a person whose job is to remove garbage.

The **trash collector** comes by once a week to pick up our garbage.

treason: (TREE-zun) *n.* the crime of doing something that harms one's government.

American soldier Benedict Arnold committed **treason** when he helped Great Britain during the War for Independence.

treaty: (TREE-tee) *n.* a formal agreement between two or more groups.

William Penn and the Lenni Lenape Indians made a **treaty** that kept peace between them for 75 years.

tree: (tree) *n.* a tall plant with a wood trunk and branches.

The leaves will fall off this **tree** in the winter.

triangle: (TRIY-ang-gul) *n.* a shape with three points.

The young girl colored the **triangle** orange.

tricycle: (TRIY-sik-ul) *n.* a vehicle that has one large front wheel and two smaller back wheels.

My little brother is learning to ride a **tricycle**.

truck: (truk) *n.* a vehicle used to carry people, goods, and materials.

He filled the back of the **truck** with plants and supplies for the garden.

truck driver: (truk DRIY-vur) *n.* a person whose job is to move goods in a truck from one place to another.

The **truck driver** is delivering supplies to the store.

truthful: (TROOTH-ful) *adj.* honest.

The boy promised to be **truthful**.

Tuesday: (TOOZ-day) *n.* the day of the week after Monday and before Wednesday.

he school is having a meeting this **Tuesday**.

turkey: (TUR-kee) *n.* a large bird with a wide feathered tail.

he farmer is raising chickens, a pig, and a **turkey**.

turn: (turn) *v.* to cause to move around a center; to rotate.

The Ferris wheel **turns** around and around.

turtle: (TURT-ul) *n.* a reptile with a shell covering the main part of its body.

he **turtle** hides inside its shell when it is frightened.

12

twelve: (twelv) *n.* a number equaling 10 plus two; numbers are usually used as adjectives in a sentence.

Mr. Gonzalez has **twelve** pencils in the desk drawer.

20

twenty: (TWEN-tee) *n.* a number equaling 10 times two; numbers are usually used as adjectives in a sentence.

Four rows of five dots make a total of **twenty** dots.

2

two: (too) *n.* a number equaling one plus one; numbers are usually used as adjectives in a sentence.

He ate **two** cupcakes for dessert.

typewriter: (TIYP-riy-tur) *n.* a machine used for writing.

He typed the letter on a **typewriter**.

tyranny: (TEER-uh-nee) *n.* government ruled by one cruel person with complete power.

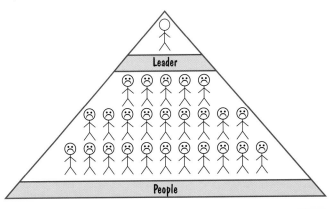

In a **tyranny**, the leader has all the power and the people have none.

Uu

ugly: (UHG-lee) *adj.* unpleasant to look at.

I drew a picture of an **ugly** monster.

umbrella: (um-BREL-uh) *n.* a covering that protects a person from rain.

I always carry an **umbrella**, just in case it rains.

uncle: (UNG-kul) *n.* the brother of one's father or mother.

John's **uncle** takes care of him when his parents go out of town.

under: (UHN-dur) *prep.* in a position below something.

The puppy is hiding **under** the table.

underneath: (uhn-dur-NEETH) *prep.* below the surface of; beneath.

The rug is **underneath** the table.

underwear: (UHN-dur-wayr) *n.* clothing worn next to the skin and under other clothing.

Seth keeps his clean **underwear** in the top drawer

unit: (YOO-nit) *n.* an amount used as a measurement.

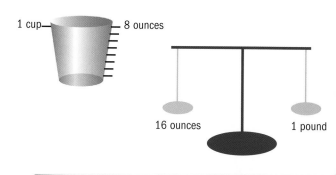

1 cup — 8 ounces

16 ounces — 1 pound

Cups, feet, ounces, and pounds are all **units** of measurement.

universe: (YOO-nuh-vurs) *n.* the planets, stars, and all things in space.

The earth is one planet in a huge **universe**.

ntil: (uhn-TIL) *prep.* up to a time.

hey stood on the beach **until** the sun went down.

up: (uhp) *prep.* in or toward a higher position.

he snail crawled **up** the stairs.

upside down: (UHP-siyd down) *prep.* in a position so that the top of something is below the bottom of it.

The monkey hung **upside down** from the tree branch.

urban: (UR-bun) *adj.* relating to a city.

These people work in an **urban** setting.

Vv

vacuum cleaner: (VAK-yoom KLEEN-ur) *n.* a machine for cleaning carpets or rugs.

Greg used the **vacuum cleaner** to clean the dirt off the floor.

van: (van) *n.* a vehicle used for carrying people and things.

The delivery man put the plants into the **van**.

VCR: (VEE-SEE-AHR) *n.* videocassette recorder; a machine for recording or playing videotapes.

We bought a **VCR** so we could watch movies at home.

vegetation: (vej-uh-TAY-shun) *n.* plant life.

The country of Ireland receives a lot of rain and is covered with **vegetation**.

vehicle: (VEE-i-kul) *n.* something used for transportation.

Cars and motorcycles are two types of **vehicles**.

velocity: (vuh-LAHS-uh-tee) *n.* the speed at which something moves.

The skier is moving at a high **velocity**.

vertical: (VUR-ti-kul) *adj.* straight up and down.

A **vertical** line allows you to separate a page into two columns.

veterinarian: (vet-ur-uh-NAYR-ee-uhn) *n.* a doctor who treats animals.

The **veterinarian** gave the puppy a shot.

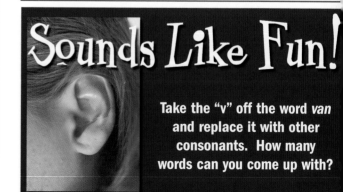

Sounds Like Fun!

Take the "v" off the word *van* and replace it with other consonants. How many words can you come up with?

veto: (VEE-toh) *v.* to forbid something when one has the authority to do so.

The president **vetoed** the bill from Congress because he did not agree with it.

videotape: (VID-ee-oh-tayp) *n.* something on which sound and pictures are recorded; videotapes can be played on a VCR.

This **videotape** shows Amy's college graduation.

volcano: (vahl-KAY-noh) *n.* a hole in the surface of the earth, through which melted rock (lava), hot ashes, and gases burst out.

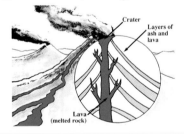

When the **volcano** called Mt. Vesuvius erupted in A.D. 79, melted rock and ash covered the entire city of Pompeii and killed all the people who lived there.

volume: (VAHL-yoom) *n.* the measured amount that a container can hold.

The **volume** of this container is 20 ounces.

voyage: (VOI-ij) *n.* a journey, especially by water, to a faraway place.

Christopher Columbus's **voyage** took him across the Atlantic Ocean.

Ww

wagon: (WAG-un) *n.* a child's toy that has four wheels and a handle.

Dave pulled his new red **wagon** all over town.

waist: (wayst) *n.* the part of the human body between the ribs and hips.

The basketball bounced up to his **waist**.

wait: (wayt) *v.* to stay until something expected happens.

We had to **wait** in line to get on the airplane.

waiter: (WAY-tur) *n.* a man who serves food in a restaurant.

The **waiter** wrote down what Jim wanted to eat and drink.

waitress: (WAY-tris) *n.* a woman who serves food in a restaurant.

The **waitress** brought the food to the table.

walk: (wawk) *v.* to move using one's feet at a natural speed.

Jerry and his dog **walk** around the neighborhood each day.

war: (wohr) *n.* a period of fighting between two groups.

During the **War** for Independence, American colonists fought against Great Britain.

warm: (wohrm) *adj.* having a medium amount of heat; not too hot, but not too cold.

We sat on the beach in the **warm** sunlight.

176

washcloth: (WAHSH-klawth) *n.* a small cloth for cleaning one's face or body.

Tyler scrubbed his face with a **washcloth**.

washing machine: (WAHSH-ing muh-SHEEN) *n.* a machine used for cleaning clothes.

Pat put the dirty clothes in the **washing machine**.

wastebasket: (WAYST-bas-kit) *n.* a container for small items of trash.

Fred put his trash in the **wastebasket**.

watch: (wahch) *v.* to look at in order to see what happens.

Myra **watched** the eggs boil in the water.

water: (WAH-tur) *n.* a clear liquid that makes up rain, lakes, and rivers.

He drinks eight glasses of **water** a day.

watermelon: (WAH-tur-mel-un) *n.* a large fruit that has a hard green skin on the outside and juicy red fruit on the inside.

We ate **watermelon** at the picnic.

wave: (wayv) *n.* moving water that rises above the surface of an ocean or other body of water.

You can see big **waves** in the Pacific Ocean.

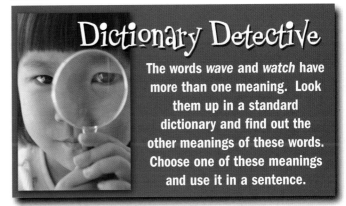

Dictionary Detective

The words *wave* and *watch* have more than one meaning. Look them up in a standard dictionary and find out the other meanings of these words. Choose one of these meanings and use it in a sentence.

177

Ww

weak: (week) *adj.* not strong.

He was too **weak** to lift the weights.

weather: (WE<u>TH</u>-ur) *n.* the temperature, rainfall, and wind conditions of a place at any given time.

MON	TUE	WED	THU	FRI
Sunny	Partly Cloudy	Mostly Cloudy, Rainy	Mostly Cloudy	Partly Cloudy
High 64°F Low 49°F	High 61°F Low 39°F	High 49°F Low 33°F	High 55°F Low 42°F	High 62°F Low 48°F

We are expecting bad **weather** on Wednesday.

web site: (web siyt) *n.* a location on the Internet containing information.

The teacher put the assignment on the class **web site**.

Wednesday: (WENZ-day) *n.* the day of the week after Tuesday and before Thursday.

We have a science test on **Wednesday**.

weight: (wayt) *n.* the measure of how heavy a person or object is.

He used the scale to find out his **weight**.

well: (wel) *adj.* in a good condition or state; healthy.

The doctor said that Rae is **well**.

west: (west) *n.* the direction opposite of east.

On most maps, **west** is to the left.

wet: (wet) *adj.* moist or soaked with liquid.

They were **wet** after playing with the water hose.

178

whale: (whayl) *n.* a large mammal with a ishlike body that lives in the ocean.

The fisherman saw a huge **whale** next to his boat.

wheel: (wheel) *n.* a round object that turns around and around.

The wheel of his car is damaged and needs to be fixed.

whistle: (WHIS-ul) *n.* an object that makes a oud sound.

She uses a **whistle** to call her dog.

white: (whiyt) *adj.* a color.

This is the color **white**.

whole: (hohl) *adj.* made up of all its parts; entire or total.

We ate a **whole** apple pie on Thanksgiving.

wide: (wiyd) *adj.* broad; not narrow.

She stretched her arms out **wide**.

width: (width) *n.* the distance from one side to another.

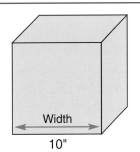

Width

10"

The **width** of this box is 10 inches.

wild: (wiyld) *adj.* not tame.

Raccoons are **wild** animals.

Ww

wildlife: (WIYLD-liyf) *n.* animals living in nature.

We studied zebras, wildebeests, and other African **wildlife**.

wind: (wind) *n.* moving air; breeze.

The **wind** made his skin feel cold and dry.

window: (WIN-doh) *n.* an opening in a building's wall that you can see through.

The sunlight comes in through the **window**.

winter: (WIN-tur) *n.* the season between fall and spring.

Jerry shovels snow in the **winter**.

wise: (wiyz) *adj.* having good judgment.

In some stories, owls are shown as **wise** animals.

with: (with) *prep.* accompanied by.

Beatrice went shopping **with** her baby.

wolf: (woolf) *n.* a wild mammal that looks like a dog.

We heard a **wolf** howling outside.

woman: (WUM-un) *n.* a female adult.

The **woman** in the blue dress is my sister.

worm: (wurm) *n.* a long, slender invertebrate (animal with no backbone).

I found a **worm** in the tomato plant.

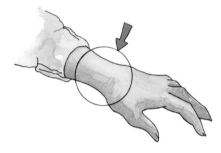

wreck: (rek) *v.* to destroy or ruin.

He **wrecked** his car when he hit a tree.

wrist: (rist) *n.* the lower part of the arm where t joins the hand.

You turn your hand by moving your **wrist**.

write: (riyt) *v.* to form letters on paper.

I decided to **write** a letter to my friend.

Xx

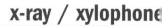

x-ray: (EKS-ray) *n.* a picture showing the bones inside a body.

The **x-ray** showed that her arm was not broken.

xylophone: (ZIY-luh-fohn) *n.* a musical instrument with bars that make sounds when you hit them.

She is learning to play the **xylophone**.

yam: (yam) *n.* a thick vegetable with orange or brown skin.

We ate **yams** with our Thanksgiving dinner.

yard: (yahrd) *n.* the ground outside a house.

The children often play in the **yard** after school.

yarn: (yahrn) *n.* a thick thread made of cotton or wool used for knitting and weaving.

I will need more **yarn** to finish knitting the blanket.

yellow: (YEL-oh) *adj.* a color.

This is the color **yellow**.

Sunday	
Monday	
Tuesday	(yesterday)
Wednesday	today
Thursday	tomorrow
Friday	
Saturday	

yesterday: (YES-tur-day) *n.* the day before today.

Yesterday I went to visit my uncle.

young: (yuhng) *adj.* being in the early stages of life.

The **young** horses stay close to their mother.

Zz

zebra: (ZEE-bruh) *n.* a large mammal with hooves and black-and-white striped fur.

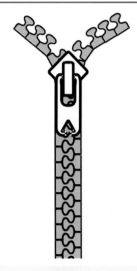

Each **zebra** has a different pattern of stripes.

zipper: (ZIP-ur) *n.* something used to fasten clothes or other items.

The **zipper** on my bag is broken, so I can't close it.

zoo: (zoo) *n.* a parklike area in which animals live and people visit.

The Ramos family saw many types of animals at the **zoo**.

zoology: (zoh-AHL-uh-gee) *n.* the study of animals.

In **zoology** class, we learned how cats and lions are related.

zucchini: (zoo-KEE-nee) *n.* a dark green vegetable.

I like **zucchini** cooked with a little butter.

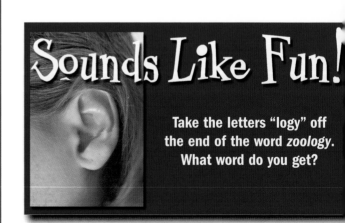

Sounds Like Fun!

Take the letters "logy" off the end of the word *zoology*. What word do you get?

Appendixes

IDIOMS

ARE WAY OVER MY HEAD!

Idioms are sayings that don't make sense on their own, but they have meaning to the people who use them. Each language and even certain cultures have their own idioms. There are lots of idioms in American English. Here's one example: Let's say you and a friend planned to go to a new movie you both really wanted to see. When you got to the movie theater, you found that the movie was sold out. There were no more tickets. You were very upset, and your friend said, "No use crying over spilled milk." Did you actually spill a glass of milk? Of course not! This idiom means that there's no point getting upset over something that has already happened and can't be changed. Here are more examples of American English idioms. Read the idioms first and see if you can guess their meanings before looking at the explanations in red.

She let the cat out of the bag.
(She gave away the secret.)

Cat got your tongue?
(Why can't you talk?)

He's just stringing her along.
(He isn't being honest with her.)

This assignment is over my head.
(I don't understand this assignment.)

Get off my back.
(Stop bothering me.)

They got their wires crossed.
(They misunderstood each other.)

I got it straight from the horse's mouth.
(A very reliable person told me.)

She spilled the beans.
(She revealed a secret.)

You don't have to jump down my throat.
(You don't have to be angry with me.)

She bit off more than she can chew.
(She took on too many
responsibilities.)

You're pulling my leg!
(You're joking!)

Let's play it by ear.
(Let's see what happens
and go from there.)

I'm washing my hands of it.
(I'm not dealing with it anymore.)

Hang on!
(Wait!)

She got up on the wrong side of the bed.
(She's in a bad mood.)

You're driving me up a wall!
(You are annoying me!)

You knocked my socks off.
(You impressed me.)

He had me in stitches.
(He made me laugh very hard.)

She's got something up her sleeve.
(She's planning something secretly.)

I'm at the end of my rope!
(I can't take it anymore!)

If the shoe fits, wear it.
(Admit the truth about yourself.)

He really blew it this time.
(He made a big mistake.)

Give it your best shot.
(Try your hardest.)

My eyes were bigger than my stomach.
(I took more food than I could eat.)

He will bend over backwards
to help you.
(He tries very hard to help.)

Don't spread yourself too thin.
(Don't get involved in too many
things at once.)

They're having trouble
making ends meet.
(They're having money problems.)

The early bird catches the worm.
(There is an advantage to being
somewhere early.)

She likes to toot her own horn.
(She likes to tell others
how wonderful she is.)

She pulled a few strings.
(She used her influence.)

187

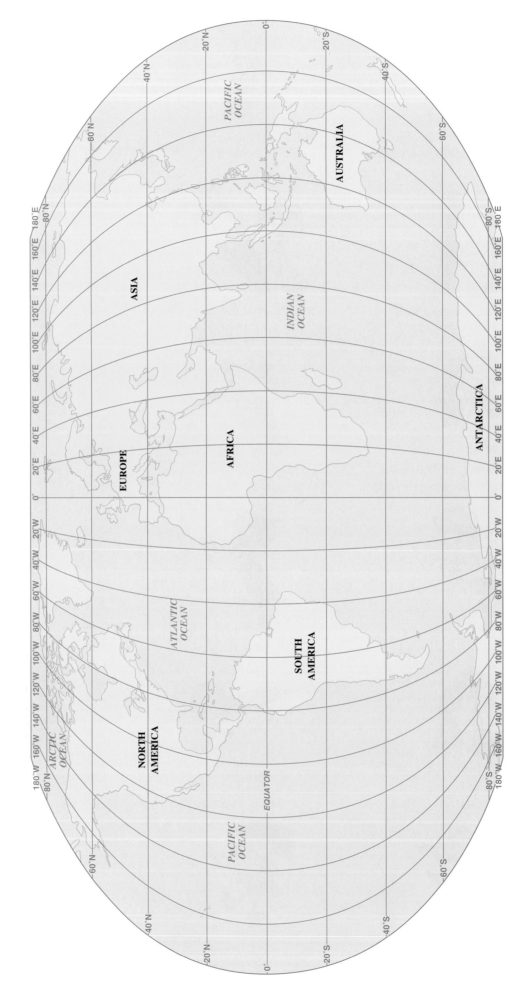

World Map

NOTE: The equator is at 0° latitude. The prime meridian is at 0° longitude.

U.S. Map

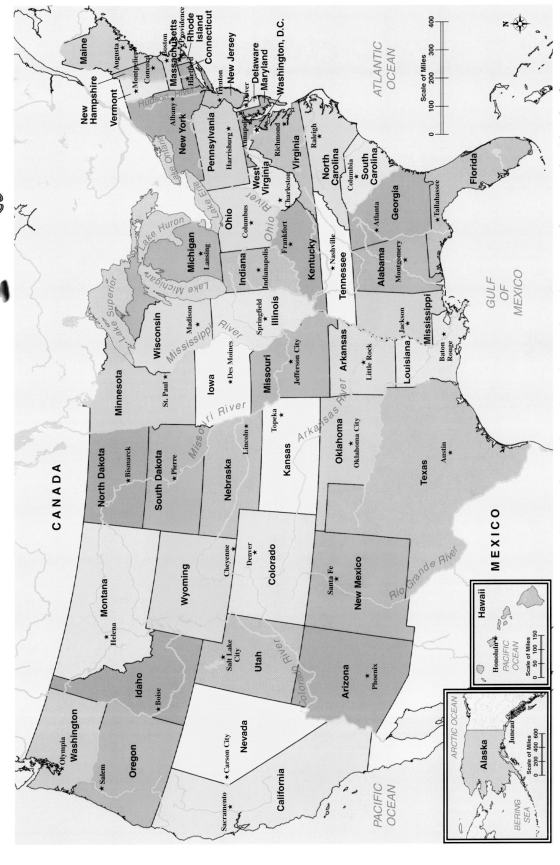

NOTE: The state of Alaska is actually located northwest of Canada and it is larger than the state of Texas. The islands of Hawaii are located nearly 3,000 miles southwest of the coast of California. See if you can locate Alaska and Hawaii on the world map. **HINT:** Alaska is located 60° N of the equator and 150° W of the prime meridian. Hawaii is located 20° N of the equator and 160° W of the prime meridian.

189

United States Presidents

In presidential elections in the United States, the person who receives the most votes may not win the election. That's because American citizens do not directly elect the president and vice president. Instead, U.S. citizens vote for people called electors who promise to vote for a particular presidential candidate. After all the citizens have voted in the election, the electors meet as the Electoral College. It is this group that actually elects the president and vice president. If a candidate does not receive a majority of votes in the Electoral College, the House of Representatives elects the president and vice president. Three times in our nation's history, the person who received the most popular votes in the election did not become president. You can read more about presidential elections below.

1 George Washington

Born: February 22, 1732
Died: December 14, 1799
Political Party: no political party
Term: 1789-97
Years in Office: 8 years
Interesting Facts: George Washington was the first president of the United States. At the First Continental Congress in 1775, Washington was elected to serve as the leader of the Continental Army. When the new constitution was approved, Washington received all the votes and was elected president because the delegates thought he was such a strong leader.

2 John Adams

Born: October 30, 1735
Died: July 4, 1826
Political Party: Federalist
Term: 1797-1801
Years in Office: 4 years
Interesting Facts: The only presidents to sign the Declaration of Independence, John Adams and Thomas Jefferson, both died on July 4, 1826, exactly 50 years later. As Adams was dying, he said, "Thomas Jefferson survives." Jefferson, however, had passed away a few hours earlier.

3 Thomas Jefferson

Born: April 13, 1743
Died: July 4, 1826
Political Party: Democratic-Republican
Term: 1801-09
Years in Office: 8 years
Interesting Facts: Thomas Jefferson wrote the Declaration of Independence. As president, he was responsible for the Louisiana Purchase, which doubled the size of the United States. He also was an inventor and architect.

4 James Madison

Born: March 16, 1751
Died: June 28, 1836
Political Party: Democratic-Republican
Term: 1809-17
Years in Office: 8 years
Interesting Facts: In 1787, James Madison helped create a new system of laws for the United States government. As a result, he became known as the "father of the Constitution." While Madison was president, the United States declared war on Great Britain and the War of 1812 began.

5 James Monroe

Born: April 28, 1758
Died: July 4, 1831
Political Party: Democratic-Republican
Term: 1817-25
Years in Office: 8 years
Interesting Facts: In the election of 1820, Monroe received every electoral vote except one. A New Hampshire delegate voted against him because the delegate wanted George Washington to be known in history as the only president to receive all the electoral votes in an election.

6 John Quincy Adams

Born: July 11, 1767
Died: February 23, 1848
Political Party: Democratic-Republican
Term: 1825-29
Years in Office: 4 years
Interesting Facts: John Quincy Adams was the first son of a president to be elected president. His opponent, Andrew Jackson, received more popular and electoral votes than Adams. However, since Jackson did not receive a majority of electoral votes, the House of Representatives was responsible for choosing the president. This caused many problems during Adams' presidency.

7 Andrew Jackson

Born: March 15, 1767
Died: June 8, 1845
Political Party: Democratic
Term: 1829-37
Years in Office: 8 years
Interesting Facts: Andrew Jackson was a general in the War of 1812. Jackson became a national hero when he defeated the British at New Orleans. Additionally, Jackson was the first president to ride on a railroad train.

Special "Political" Vocabulary

candidate: a person who is running for a political office

delegate: a person who has the power to act for someone else

elector: a member of the Electoral College

Electoral College: a group of delegates who have been chosen by the states and the District of Columbia to elect the president and vice president

electoral vote: a vote by a member of the Electoral College

inauguration: the formal ceremony in which the person who was elected president takes the oath of office; during this ceremony, the president gives a speech called the "inaugural address"

popular vote: a vote by a citizen

scandal: a situation in which someone or something has caused shame or embarrassment

8 Martin Van Buren

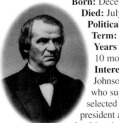

Born: December 5, 1782
Died: July 24, 1862
Political Party: Democratic
Term: 1837-41
Years in Office: 4 years
Interesting Facts: Martin Van Buren was from Kinderhook, New York. He was sometimes referred to as Old Kinderhook or O.K. when people talked or wrote about him. Later, "O.K." came to mean "all right," thus creating the term okay." Van Buren was against slavery and ran unsuccessfully for president in 1848 as a member of the Free Soil Party.

9 William Henry Harrison

Born: February 9, 1773
Died: April 4, 1841
Political Party: Whig
Term: 1841
Years in Office: 1 month
Interesting Facts: Soon after he was elected president, William Henry Harrison gave a speech that lasted almost two hours as part of his inauguration. It was an extremely cold day and Harrison did not wear a hat. He became sick with pneumonia and died in the White House one month later. His father, Benjamin Harrison, signed the Declaration of Independence.

10 John Tyler

Born: March 29, 1790
Died: January 18, 1862
Political Party: Whig
Term: 1841-45
Years in Office: 3 years, 11 months
Interesting Facts: John Tyler was originally a Democrat, but he was nominated by the Whig Party to run with Harrison. When he became president, he did not support some of the policies the Whigs favored and was not well liked by the party. Because John Tyler joined the Confederacy 20 years after his presidency, he is the only president to be named an enemy of the United States.

11 James Polk

Born: November 2, 1795
Died: June 15, 1849
Political Party: Democratic
Term: 1845-49
Years in Office: 4 years
Interesting Facts: As president, James Polk expanded the territory of the United States. He gained part of the Oregon Territory from the British. After a short war with Mexico, he purchased territory from that country for $15,000,000. This territory included the current states of California, New Mexico, Arizona, and Utah, and small parts of Colorado, Wyoming, Kansas, and Oklahoma.

12 Zachary Taylor

Born: November 24, 1784
Died: July 9, 1850
Political Party: Whig
Term: 1849-50
Years in Office: 1 year, 4 months, 5 days
Interesting Facts: Zachary Taylor and James Madison were second cousins. Taylor got the nickname "Old Rough and Ready" during the Seminole War in 1838. He was a popular military leader in the Mexican War. Taylor died in office on July 9, 1850. People believed he died from poisoning, but research in the early 1990s disproved this theory.

13 Millard Fillmore

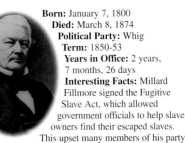

Born: January 7, 1800
Died: March 8, 1874
Political Party: Whig
Term: 1850-53
Years in Office: 2 years, 7 months, 26 days
Interesting Facts: Millard Fillmore signed the Fugitive Slave Act, which allowed government officials to help slave owners find their escaped slaves. This upset many members of his party and they did not want him to represent their party in the next election. During his presidency, Fillmore opened trade between the United States and Japan.

14 Franklin Pierce

Born: November 23, 1804
Died: October 8, 1869
Political Party: Democratic
Term: 1853-57
Years in Office: 4 years
Interesting Facts: Franklin Pierce memorized his 3,319-word inaugural speech and did not use any notes. He is the only president to say "I promise" instead of "I swear" when he took office. He did this for religious reasons. Pierce also encouraged the building of the railroad across the United States, and he purchased territory from Mexico.

15 James Buchanan

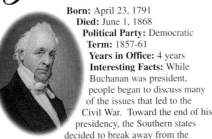

Born: April 23, 1791
Died: June 1, 1868
Political Party: Democratic
Term: 1857-61
Years in Office: 4 years
Interesting Facts: While Buchanan was president, people began to discuss many of the issues that led to the Civil War. Toward the end of his presidency, the Southern states decided to break away from the Union. Although Buchanan opposed the abolitionists, he remained loyal to the Union after the Civil War started. James Buchanan was the only president who never married.

16 Abraham Lincoln

Born: February 12, 1809
Died: April 15, 1865
Political Party: Republican
Term: 1861-65
Years in Office: 4 years, 1 month, 10 days
Interesting Facts: Before Abraham Lincoln was inaugurated on March 4, 1861, seven states had broken away from the Union. The Civil War began only a few weeks after Lincoln became president. During the war, Lincoln signed the Emancipation Proclamation, freeing the slaves in the Southern states that were at war with the Union. In 1865, five days after the South's surrender, Lincoln was shot by an assassin named John Wilkes Booth.

17 Andrew Johnson

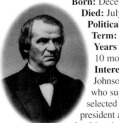

Born: December 29, 1808
Died: July 31, 1875
Political Party: Democratic
Term: 1865-69
Years in Office: 3 years, 10 months, 20 days
Interesting Facts: Andrew Johnson, a Southern Democrat who supported the Union, was selected as Lincoln's vice president and became president after Lincoln was assassinated. After the Civil War, some Republicans in Congress thought that he was not being strict enough. They thought a new form of slavery was being established in the South. Eventually, Congress impeached Johnson. The Senate voted on whether or not to remove him from office. They were one vote short of the required two-thirds votes necessary to remove him from office.

18 Ulysses S. Grant

Born: April 27, 1822
Died: July 23, 1885
Political Party: Republican
Term: 1869-77
Years in Office: 8 years
Interesting Facts: Ulysses Grant graduated from West Point and served in the Mexican War, for which he was recognized for his bravery. He left the U.S. Army in 1854. When the Civil War began, he returned to the army. He captured the city of Vicksburg in 1863 and was appointed commander of the Union army. Grant was responsible for many Union victories in the war. General Robert E. Lee, a Confederate general, surrendered to him on April 9, 1865, ending the Civil War.

19 Rutherford B. Hayes

Born: October 4, 1822
Died: January 17, 1893
Political Party: Republican
Term: 1877-81
Years in Office: 4 years
Interesting Facts: Rutherford B. Hayes received fewer popular votes than his opponent. After many problems, he was named the winner of the election because he had the most electoral votes. The election was decided on March 2, 1877, two days before he was sworn in as president. Hayes and his wife, Lucy, did not allow any alcohol in the White House. Because of this, the First Lady was nicknamed "Lemonade Lucy."

20 James A. Garfield

Born: November 19, 1831
Died: September 19, 1881
Political Party: Republican
Term: 1881
Years in Office: 6 months, 15 days
Interesting Facts: James Garfield won the election with 48.5% of the popular vote. His opponent had 48.1% of the popular vote. Garfield could write Latin with one hand and Greek with the other. He was assassinated and died on September 19, 1881.

21 Chester A. Arthur

Born: October 5, 1829*
Died: November 18, 1886
Political Party: Republican
Term: 1881-85
Years in Office: 3 years, 5 months, 15 days
Interesting Facts: A year into his presidency, Chester Arthur found out that he had a deadly kidney disease. He did not let this affect his work as president and became greatly respected.

*Historians disagree on the year of Arthur's birth. Some sources say October 5, 1830.

22 Grover Cleveland

Born: March 18, 1837
Died: June 24, 1908
Political Party: Democratic
Term: 1885-89
Years in Office: 4 years
Interesting Facts: Grover Cleveland was the first president since the Civil War who had not served in the military during the war. The government asked him to serve in the military, but he hired a substitute to take his place, a practice that was permitted at that time. Cleveland is the only president who got married while he was president.

23 Benjamin Harrison

Born: August 20, 1833
Died: March 13, 1901
Political Party: Republican
Term: 1889-93
Years in Office: 4 years
Interesting Facts: Benjamin Harrison signed the Sherman Antitrust Act into law. He invited officials from North and South America to attend the First Pan-American Congress in Washington, D.C. in 1889. He was the grandson of the ninth president, William Henry Harrison.

24 Grover Cleveland

Born: March 18, 1837
Died: June 24, 1908
Political Party: Democratic
Term: 1893-97
Years in Office: 4 years
Interesting Facts: Grover Cleveland served two complete terms as president, but the terms were not in a row. When Cleveland became president in 1893, he put the queen of Hawaii, who had been removed from office, back in power.

25 William McKinley

Born: January 29, 1843
Died: September 14, 1901
Political Party: Republican
Term: 1897-1901
Years in Office: 4 years, 6 months, 5 days
Interesting Facts: When problems arose between Spain and Cuba, William McKinley sent the battleship *Maine* to Havana, Cuba's capital city. An explosion destroyed the *Maine* and the United States declared war on Spain. McKinley sent the U.S. Navy to attack Spanish territory in Cuba and the Philippines. The Spanish navy was destroyed and a peace treaty was signed. He was assassinated and died on September 14, 1901.

26 Theodore Roosevelt

Born: October 27, 1858
Died: January 6, 1919
Political Party: Republican
Term: 1901-09
Years in Office: 7 years, 5 months, 21 days
Interesting Facts: Theodore "Teddy" Roosevelt was a sickly child who overcame many childhood illnesses to become a well-loved president. Roosevelt was not afraid to use the power of the presidency. He directed the building of the Panama Canal, which connected the Caribbean Sea to the Pacific Ocean. The Teddy Bear was named after Roosevelt when he refused to kill an injured bear while he was on a hunting trip.

27 William H. Taft

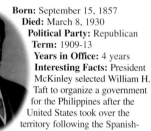

Born: September 15, 1857
Died: March 8, 1930
Political Party: Republican
Term: 1909-13
Years in Office: 4 years
Interesting Facts: President McKinley selected William H. Taft to organize a government for the Philippines after the United States took over the territory following the Spanish-American War. After Taft, a lawyer, left the presidency, President Harding appointed him Chief Justice of the Supreme Court. On this honor, Taft commented, "I don't remember that I ever was president."

28 Woodrow Wilson

Born: December 28, 1856
Died: February 3, 1924
Political Party: Democratic
Term: 1913-21
Years in Office: 8 years
Interesting Facts: Woodrow Wilson was a college professor and president of Princeton University before being elected president of the United States. When World War I started in Europe, Wilson tried to keep the United States out of the war. However, in 1917, he asked Congress to declare war on Germany and the countries supporting Germany. He said that the war was being fought "to make the world safe for democracies." Despite his involvement in the war, he was known as a man of peace.

29 Warren G. Harding

Born: November 2, 1865
Died: August 2, 1923
Political Party: Republican
Term: 1921-23
Years in Office: 2 years, 4 months, 7 days
Interesting Facts: Warren Harding was the first president to own a radio and to speak on the radio. Many of his friends used their political positions to make money for themselves. Harding was upset by this and was not sure if he should keep this secret or tell people the truth. He died from poisoning in San Francisco before deciding what to do about the scandal.

30 Calvin Coolidge

Born: July 4, 1872
Died: January 5, 1933
Political Party: Republican
Term: 1923-29
Years in Office: 5 years, 7 months, 4 days
Interesting Facts: Calvin Coolidge, nicknamed "Silent Cal" because he did not speak very much, was once told by a woman that she had made a bet that she could get more than three words out of him in conversation. His reply? "You lose."

31 Herbert Hoover

Born: August 10, 1874
Died: October 20, 1964
Political Party: Republican
Term: 1929-33
Years in Office: 4 years
Interesting Facts: While many people blame Herbert Hoover for the Great Depression, the events leading up to it began long before he came to office. Before his term, he worked to bring food and other help to suffering people around the world. He arranged shipments of food to starving people in Russia, saying, "Twenty million people are starving. Whatever their politics, they shall be fed!"

32 Franklin D. Roosevelt

Born: January 30, 1882
Died: April 12, 1945
Political Party: Democratic
Term: 1933-45
Years in Office: 12 years, 1 month, 18 days
Interesting Facts: When Franklin Roosevelt was 39, he found out that he had polio, a disease that caused him to lose his ability to stand or walk without heavy braces on his legs. In private, he used a wheelchair. Although he tried to keep the United States from getting involved in World War II, after Japan attacked Pearl Harbor, Roosevelt declared war on Japan and the countries supporting Japan. Roosevelt also helped America out of the Great Depression. His cousin Theodore Roosevelt was the 26th president.

33 Harry S Truman

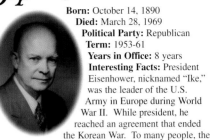

Born: May 8, 1884
Died: December 26, 1972
Political Party: Democratic
Term: 1945-53
Years in Office: 7 years, 9 months, 9 days
Interesting Facts: Though many people remember Harry Truman for his order to drop the atomic bombs on Hiroshima and Nagasaki, Japan, he was responsible for many acts of peace. Among these were his plans to help rebuild Europe after World War II. Truman had a saying: "The Buck Stops Here." He believed that a president should take responsibility for everything that happens during his term in office.

34 Dwight D. Eisenhower

Born: October 14, 1890
Died: March 28, 1969
Political Party: Republican
Term: 1953-61
Years in Office: 8 years
Interesting Facts: President Eisenhower, nicknamed "Ike," was the leader of the U.S. Army in Europe during World War II. While president, he reached an agreement that ended the Korean War. To many people, the most memorable action he took while in office was to send National Guard troops to Little Rock, Arkansas, to make sure that black children were allowed to attend the same schools as white children.

35 John F. Kennedy

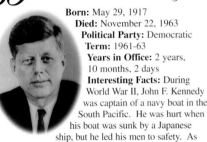

Born: May 29, 1917
Died: November 22, 1963
Political Party: Democratic
Term: 1961-63
Years in Office: 2 years, 10 months, 2 days
Interesting Facts: During World War II, John F. Kennedy was captain of a navy boat in the South Pacific. He was hurt when his boat was sunk by a Japanese ship, but he led his men to safety. As president, Kennedy called for an end to the separate treatment of people of different races. He also prevented Russia from setting up missiles in Cuba. He was the first president to send military advisors to South Vietnam. He was assassinated on November 22, 1963.

36 Lyndon B. Johnson

Born: August 27, 1908
Died: January 22, 1973
Political Party: Democratic
Term: 1963-69
Years in Office: 5 years, 1 month, 29 days
Interesting Facts: Lyndon B. Johnson's first acts as president were to complete the work Kennedy had started before he was killed, including getting Congress to pass the Civil Rights Act. During his early years in Texas, Johnson taught students from Mexican families. Many believe his interest in helping minorities went back to that early experience. He is also remembered for greatly increasing America's involvement in the Vietnam War.

37 Richard M. Nixon

Born: January 9, 1913
Died: April 22, 1994
Political Party: Republican
Term: 1969-74
Years in Office: 5 years, 6 months, 20 days
Interesting Facts: Richard Nixon was vice president under Eisenhower. He ran for, but lost the presidency in 1960. He ran again and was elected president in 1968. Nixon is recognized for his work in opening diplomatic relations between the United States and China. He left the presidency on August 9, 1974 as a result of a scandal involving political spying and a burglary at the Watergate Hotel in Washington, D.C.

38 Gerald R. Ford

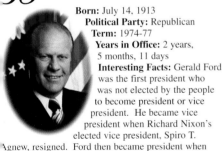

Born: July 14, 1913
Political Party: Republican
Term: 1974-77
Years in Office: 2 years, 5 months, 11 days
Interesting Facts: Gerald Ford was the first president who was not elected by the people to become president or vice president. He became vice president when Richard Nixon's elected vice president, Spiro T. Agnew, resigned. Ford then became president when Nixon resigned.

39 Jimmy Carter

Born: October 1, 1924
Political Party: Democratic
Term: 1977-81
Years in Office: 4 years
Interesting Facts: After Jimmy Carter was inaugurated president, he walked from the Capitol to the White House to show that he was a common man. As president, Carter tried to make peace in the Middle East. He continued to work for world peace even after his presidency. He was awarded the Nobel Prize for peace in 2002 for his work in improving the lives of people all over the world.

40 Ronald W. Reagan

Born: February 6, 1911
Died: June 5, 2004
Political Party: Republican
Term: 1981-89
Years in Office: 8 years
Interesting Facts: Ronald Reagan was a Hollywood actor in the 1950s before he became interested in politics. He successfully ran for governor of California before winning two terms as president of the United States. Reagan helped put an end to the Cold War between the United States and what was the Soviet Union. He has not appeared in public since he announced that he has Alzheimer's disease in the early 1990s.

41 George H. W. Bush

Born: June 12, 1924
Political Party: Republican
Term: 1989-93
Years in Office: 4 years
Interesting Facts: George Bush served as a fighter pilot in the Pacific during World War II. He was elected president after serving as Ronald Reagan's vice president for eight years. In 1990, Iraq invaded Kuwait because of a disagreement over money. In January 1991, the U.S. Congress voted to allow President Bush to use force against Iraq, thus beginning the Persian Gulf War. During his presidency, Bush signed a law making the late Dr. Martin Luther King, Jr.'s birthday a national holiday.

42 William J. Clinton

Born: August 19, 1946
Political Party: Democratic
Term: 1993-2001
Years in Office: 8 years
Interesting Facts: William "Bill" Clinton was the first Democratic president to serve two terms since Franklin Roosevelt. He tried to bring a lasting peace in the Middle East. During his eight years in office, many people in the United States enjoyed great economic success. Clinton was impeached in 1998 because of a White House scandal. The Senate voted on whether or not to remove him from office, but they did not get the two-thirds votes required.

43 George W. Bush

Born: July 6, 1946
Political Party: Republican
Term: 2001-present
Years in Office: 2001-present
Interesting Facts: The son of George H. W. Bush, George W. Bush was the second son of a president to be elected president. He received fewer popular votes than his opponent, but was declared the winner with the most electoral votes after the U.S. Supreme Court overturned the Florida Supreme Court's ruling on recounting ballots. When terrorists killed thousands of Americans on September 11, 2001, Bush declared a war on terrorism.

U.S. State Facts

ALABAMA
Capital: Montgomery
Area: 51,718 square miles
Statehood: December 14, 1819

ALASKA
Capital: Juneau
Area: 587,878 square miles
Statehood: January 3, 1959

ARIZONA
Capital: Phoenix
Area: 114,007 square miles
Statehood: February 14, 1912

ARKANSAS
Capital: Little Rock
Area: 53,183 square miles
Statehood: June 15, 1836

CALIFORNIA
Capital: Sacramento
Area: 158,648 square miles
Statehood: September 9, 1850

COLORADO
Capital: Denver
Area: 104,100 square miles
Statehood: August 1, 1876

CONNECTICUT
Capital: Hartford
Area: 5,006 square miles
Statehood: January 9, 1788

DELAWARE
Capital: Dover
Area: 2,026 square miles
Statehood: December 7, 1787

FLORIDA
Capital: Tallahassee
Area: 58,681 square miles
Statehood: March 3, 1845

GEORGIA
Capital: Atlanta
Area: 58,930 square miles
Statehood: January 2, 1788

HAWAII
Capital: Honolulu
Area: 6,459 square miles
Statehood: August 21, 1959

IDAHO
Capital: Boise
Area: 83,574 square miles
Statehood: July 3, 1890

ILLINOIS
Capital: Springfield
Area: 57,343 square miles
Statehood: December 3, 1818

INDIANA
Capital: Indianapolis
Area: 36,185 square miles
Statehood: December 11, 1816

IOWA
Capital: Des Moines
Area: 56,276 square miles
Statehood: December 28, 1846

KANSAS
Capital: Topeka
Area: 82,282 square miles
Statehood: January 29, 1861

KENTUCKY
Capital: Frankfort
Area: 40,411 square miles
Statehood: June 1, 1792

LOUISIANA
Capital: Baton Rouge
Area: 47,717 square miles
Statehood: April 30, 1812

MAINE
Capital: Augusta
Area: 33,128 square miles
Statehood: March 15, 1820

MARYLAND
Capital: Annapolis
Area: 10,455 square miles
Statehood: April 28, 1788

MASSACHUSETTS
Capital: Boston
Area: 8,262 square miles
Statehood: February 6, 1788

MICHIGAN
Capital: Lansing
Area: 58,513 square miles
Statehood: January 26, 1837

MINNESOTA
Capital: St. Paul
Area: 84,397 square miles
Statehood: May 11, 1858

MISSISSIPPI
Capital: Jackson
Area: 47,698 square miles
Statehood: December 10, 1817

MISSOURI
Capital: Jefferson City
Area: 69,709 square miles
Statehood: August 10, 1821

MONTANA
Capital: Helena
Area: 147,047 square miles
Statehood: November 8, 1889

NEBRASKA
Capital: Lincoln
Area: 77,359 square miles
Statehood: March 1, 1867

NEVADA
Capital: Carson City
Area: 110,567 square miles
Statehood: October 31, 1864

NEW HAMPSHIRE
Capital: Concord
Area: 9,283 square miles
Statehood: June 21, 1788

NEW JERSEY
Capital: Trenton
Area: 7,790 square miles
Statehood: December 18, 1787

NEW MEXICO
Capital: Santa Fe
Area: 121,599 square miles
Statehood: January 6, 1912

NEW YORK
Capital: Albany
Area: 49,112 square miles
Statehood: July 26, 1788

NORTH CAROLINA
Capital: Raleigh
Area: 52,672 square miles
Statehood: November 21, 1789

NORTH DAKOTA
Capital: Bismarck
Area: 70,704 square miles
Statehood: November 2, 1889

OHIO
Capital: Columbus
Area: 41,328 square miles
Statehood: March 1, 1803

OKLAHOMA
Capital: Oklahoma City
Area: 69,903 square miles
Statehood: November 16, 1907

OREGON
Capital: Salem
Area: 97,052 square miles
Statehood: February 14, 1859

PENNSYLVANIA
Capital: Harrisburg
Area: 45,310 square miles
Statehood: December 12, 1787

RHODE ISLAND
Capital: Providence
Area: 1,213 square miles
Statehood: May 29, 1790

SOUTH CAROLINA
Capital: Columbia
Area: 31,117 square miles
Statehood: May 23, 1788

SOUTH DAKOTA
Capital: Pierre
Area: 77,122 square miles
Statehood: November 2, 1889

TENNESSEE
Capital: Nashville
Area: 42,146 square miles
Statehood: June 1, 1796

TEXAS
Capital: Austin
Area: 266,874 square miles
Statehood: December 29, 1845

UTAH
Capital: Salt Lake City
Area: 84,905 square miles
Statehood: January 4, 1896

VERMONT
Capital: Montpelier
Area: 9,615 square miles
Statehood: March 4, 1791

VIRGINIA
Capital: Richmond
Area: 40,598 square miles
Statehood: June 25, 1788

WASHINGTON
Capital: Olympia
Area: 68,126 square miles
Statehood: November 11, 1889

WEST VIRGINIA
Capital: Charleston
Area: 24,231 square miles
Statehood: June 20, 1863

WISCONSIN
Capital: Madison
Area: 56,145 square miles
Statehood: May 29, 1848

WYOMING
Capital: Cheyenne
Area: 97,818 square miles
Statehood: July 10, 1890

The Solar System

Our solar system is made up of nine known planets. These planets revolve around the sun. The planets are in the following order, from the one closest to the sun to the one farthest from it: Mercury, Venus, Earth, Mars, Jupiter, Saturn, Uranus, Neptune, and Pluto. A good way to remember this is through a mnemonic (see page 109 of your dictionary for a definition) such as <u>M</u>y <u>V</u>ery <u>E</u>xcellent <u>M</u>other <u>J</u>ust <u>S</u>erved <u>U</u>s <u>N</u>utritious <u>P</u>ears. Below is some information about each planet.

1. **Mercury:** *closest to the sun; second-smallest planet; no atmosphere; temperature is very hot during the day and extremely cold at night*

2. **Venus:** *closest to earth; covered in clouds and very hot*

3. **Earth:** *the only planet with liquid water on the surface; scientists think it is the only planet with tectonic activity*

4. **Mars:** *called the "red planet" because its surface has a reddish color*

5. **Jupiter:** *the largest planet in our solar system; it has many moons*

6. **Saturn:** *second largest planet in our solar system; famous for its rings (made up mostly of ice and rocks)*

7. **Uranus:** *discovered in 1781; first planet to be observed by telescope*

8. **Neptune:** *has eight known moons; surface winds clocked at 1,500 miles per hour*

9. **Pluto:** *farthest from the sun; smallest planet*

Parts of the Earth

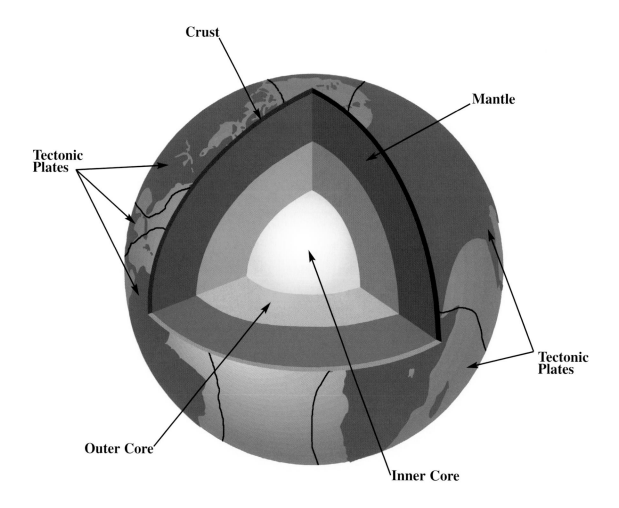

Crust

Mantle

Tectonic Plates

Tectonic Plates

Outer Core

Inner Core

Tectonic Plates: large pieces of the earth's crust
Crust: rock that is 4-25 miles thick
Mantle: heavy, rocklike materials about 1,700 miles thick
Outer Core: melted iron and nickel about 1,400 miles thick
Inner Core: solid ball of iron and nickel about 1,500 miles across

Geometric Shapes

Circle

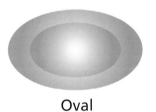
Oval

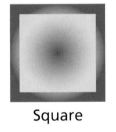
Square

Rectangle

Triangle

Parallelogram

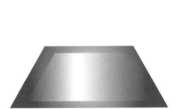
Rhombus

Trapezoid

Pentagon

Hexagon

Octagon

Cylinder

Cone

197

Units of Measurement

U.S. System	Metric System
1 ounce	28.35 grams
1 pound	.4536 kilograms
1 cup	236.59 milliliters
1 pint	.4732 liters
1 quart	.9464 liters
1 gallon	3.785 liters
1 inch	2.54 centimeters
1 foot	.3048 meters
1 yard	.9144 meters
1 mile	1.609 kilometers
98.6° Fahrenheit	37° Celsius

Roman & Arabic

N U M E R A L S

Roman	Arabic	Roman	Arabic
I	1	LX	60
II	2	LXX	70
III	3	LXXX	80
IV	4	XC	90
V	5	C	100
VI	6	CC	200
VII	7	CCC	300
VIII	8	CD	400
IX	9	D	500
X	10	DC	600
XX	20	DCC	700
XXX	30	DCCC	800
XL	40	CM	900
L	50	M	1,000

A Letter to Teachers and Parents

Learning new words can be challenging for English language learners and emerging readers, but give them a picture that illustrates the word, and the task becomes much easier. The *IDEA Picture Dictionary 2* introduces students to basic nouns, verbs, prepositions, adjectives, and content words*, and gives them a foundation of dictionary and word attack skills.

The *IDEA Picture Dictionary 2* is easy to use. Entries are organized alphabetically. Each entry word is accompanied by a picture that illustrates the word, a phonetic spelling, the part of speech, a definition, and a sentence with the word used in context. Throughout the dictionary you will find "Sounds Like Fun!" activities to build students' understanding of sounds, and "Dictionary Detective" activities to help students put their dictionary skills to work.

Using the *IDEA Picture Dictionary 2*

The *IDEA Picture Dictionary 2* is designed for intermediate to advanced English language learners and emerging readers. It can be used on its own or in conjunction with any English language development or language arts program, including *Carousel of IDEAS* and *IDEAS for Literature*.

To familiarize students with the dictionary, review "How to Use This Dictionary" on pages 4 and 5 with them. Point out the main features of the dictionary. Then go over "Here's the Key!" on pages 6 and 7. Go over each vowel and consonant sound. Read some of the "Dictionary Detective" and "Sounds Like Fun!" activities and do them together. You also can visit the web site noted below to find fun and engaging downloadable activity sheets.

Internet Link to Language Development Activities

Visit **www.ballard-tighe.com/dictionaryactivities** for links to downloadable activity sheets you can use with the *IDEA Picture Dictionary 2*. You will find fun activities designed for emerging readers and students at various stages of English language acquisition.

*Many words have multiple meanings. In most cases, only one meaning of the word has been defined in the *IDEA Picture Dictionary 2*. The meaning defined is the one most likely to be used in an academic setting. "Dictionary Detective" activities encourage students to look up alternate meanings of some words in a standard dictionary. This helps give students the skills and confidence they need to access a standard dictionary.

Art Credits

Special thanks to each artist and art source whose work is featured in this dictionary. Every effort has been made to trace copyright holders, and we apologize in advance for any omissions. We would be pleased to insert the appropriate acknowledgment in any subsequent edition of this book.

Contributing Artists

Ronaldo Benaraw
Gina Capaldi
Jeff Fillbach

Sabrina Lammé
Edith Leiby
Keith Neely

Fred Sherman
Leilani Trollinger

Art Sources

The American Revolution: A Picture Sourcebook (Dover Publications): independent, liberty
Kristin Belsher: ancient
Corbis: achieve, alike, ashamed, bone, cloud, command, concern, convince, curious, disappear, drive, economy, election, finish, foreign, fossil, fuel, geologist, guilt, heat, hurricane, irritate, jury, justice, locate, manufacture, neglect, neighborhood, obstacle, orchestra, patience, plan, rainfall, reaction, respond, responsibility, same, skeleton, soil, sorrow, sour, succeed, suspicious, symbol, thirsty, wait, weight
Creatas: audience
Dictionary of American Portraits (Dover Publications): impeach, president, treason
Dodd, Mead and Company. 1902. *History of the World*: drama
Dover Clipart Series: assassinate
Freestockphotos.com: constellation
Getty: citizen, clean, cold, collect, color, comedy, patriotism, refugee, smog
Grand Canyon Explorer, www.kaibab.org: plateau
Anne Laskey: ruins
Leslie Ley: damage
Library of Congress: abolitionist, amendment, civil war, constitution, contemporary, freedom, immigrant, peacefully, play, queen, reputation, treaty, war
Allison Mangrum: act, architecture, ceremony, construct, lie, old, wave
Michaelia Mendoza: act
National Park Service: above
Larry Newton: rice
Northwind Picture Archives: feudalism, great, voyage
pdimages.com: DNA
Dorothy Roberts: adobe, elephant, giraffe, lion, monkey, ostrich, rhinoceros, zebra
Nicholas Stathis: artifact
Roberta Stathis: theme
Tom Sullivan, www.geocities.com/paris/4118/index.html: cape

United States Presidents Appendix Art Sources

George Bush Presidential Library and Museum: George H. W. Bush
Gerald R. Ford Library: Gerald Ford
Images of American Political History, http://teachpol.tcnj.edu/amer_pol_hist/ use: George Washington, John Adams, Thomas Jefferson, James Monroe
Jimmy Carter Library and Museum: Jimmy Carter
Library of Congress: James Madison, John Quincy Adams, Andrew Jackson, Martin Van Buren, William Henry Harrison, John Tyler, James Polk, Zachary Taylor, Millard Fillmore, Franklin Pierce, James Buchanan, Andrew Johnson, Ulysses S. Grant, Rutherford B. Hayes, James Garfield, Chester Arthur, Grover Cleveland, Benjamin Harrison, William McKinley, Theodore Roosevelt, William Taft, Woodrow Wilson, Warren Harding, Calvin Coolidge, Herbert Hoover, Franklin D. Roosevelt, Harry S Truman, Dwight D. Eisenhower, John F. Kennedy, Richard Nixon
Lyndon B. Johnson Library, photo by Yoichi R. Okamoto: Lyndon B. Johnson
National Archives and Records Administration: Abraham Lincoln
Ronald Reagan Presidential Library: Ronald Reagan
White House Photo Department: George W. Bush, Presidential Seal
William Jefferson Clinton Presidential Library and Museum: William J. Clinton